JOURNEY
of the
SOUL

"Bill and Kristi Gaultiere have written an inspiring and practical book that brings together the faith and feelings aspects of spiritual formation. It is clear that they have lived what they write about, for many of the illustrations are personal. I was especially struck by the section on The Wall—the stage where we "hit the wall" in our faith—and the resolution of this coming through the Inner Journey. Every believer will have a fresh understanding of their faith development from reading this book."

David Stoop, PhD, clinical psychologist, host of New Life Radio,
and author of Forgiving What You'll Never Forget

"How many followers of Jesus have asked themselves, 'Is this all there is?' *Journey of the Soul* answers, 'There is so much more!' As experienced travel guides, Bill and Kristi help you locate where you are and how to progress in your walk. They guide you through the stages of the CHRIST journey, providing plenty of trail markers, practical suggestions, exercises, and packing lists for the next step on your journey of grace. This book is a must-read for anyone who wants to keep going and growing in Christ."

Rob Jacobs, pastor of spiritual growth, Saddleback Church

"*Journey of the Soul* by Bill and Kristi Gaultiere is well written, a most helpful and deep guide to emotional and spiritual growth based on their CHRIST stages model that is circular and nonlinear. They effectively use Scripture and quotations and stories of well-known authors such as Teresa of Avila, John of the Cross, A. W. Tozer, Frank Laubach, C. S. Lewis, Henri Nouwen, and especially Dallas Willard. They share their own experiences along with practical exercises and spiritual disciplines to be practiced in a grace-filled and non-legalistic way. This is a must-read for all of us who want to know the triune God more deeply and grow to become more like Jesus. Highly recommended!"

Siang-Yang Tan, PhD, professor of clinical psychology,
Fuller Seminary; senior pastor, First Evangelical Church
Glendale (CA); and author of Shepherding God's People

"Many people get lost or stuck on the path of personal growth, but *Journey of the Soul* gives you a map. Bill and Kristi Gaultiere have counseled us and our church for many years. In their new book, they come alongside you at each stage of faith to show you that the Lord Jesus is your friend. You'll discover new possibilities for living with love for God, yourself, and others."

Bobby and Hannah Schuller, pastors of *The Hour of Power*

"I love how the uniqueness of Bill and Kristi's personal stories complement the ways God works differently in each of us. Through their years of experience in journeying with others, they help us recognize where we are on the path of life and how the perfect qualities of Jesus are available to us. You'll be greatly encouraged as God through the Holy Spirit imparts grace for your continued growth to be ever more like Jesus."

Judy TenElshof, PhD, professor of spirituality and marriage and family, Talbot Seminary; founder, Hilltop Renewal Center

"This is a thorough, practical, and biblically infused guide to developing a deeper spiritual life. The Gaultieres lead the reader through examples of life change, self-reflection, inspiration, and application with the goal of growing our souls. This book is packed with insights for your journey and will especially speak to church attenders, pastors, and missionaries."

Ted Esler, PhD, president, Missio Nexus

JOURNEY
of the
SOUL

A Practical Guide to
Emotional and Spiritual Growth

BILL AND KRISTI GAULTIERE

Revell

a division of Baker Publishing Group
Grand Rapids, Michigan

Published by Revell
a division of Baker Publishing Group
PO Box 6287, Grand Rapids, MI 49516-6287
www.revellbooks.com

Printed in the United States of America

Library of Congress Cataloging-in-Publication Data
Names: Gaultiere, William, author. | Gaultiere, Kristi, author.
Title: Journey of the soul : a practical guide to emotional and spiritual growth / Bill & Kristi Gaultiere.
Description: Grand Rapids, Michigan : Revell, a division of Baker Publishing Group, [2021] | Includes bibliographical references.
Identifiers: LCCN 2020035382 | ISBN 9780800740351 (casebound) | ISBN 9780800739027 (paperback)
Subjects: LCSH: Spiritual life—Christianity. | Spiritual formation.
Classification: LCC BV4501.3 .G385 2021 | DDC 248—dc23
LC record available at https://lccn.loc.gov/2020035382

The authors are represented by the literary agency of The Gates Group Agency.

21 22 23 24 25 26 27   7 6 5 4 3 2 1

For everyone who has participated
in our Soul Shepherding Institute.
Thank you for sharing
the journey of your soul with us.

Contents

Acknowledgments

Publishing this book took seven years. We experienced many rejections and did many rewrites. We persevered because of help from Jesus and some key friends.

First, there were encouragements from Dallas Willard. One day over lunch he surprised me: "Bill, I feel impressed to ask what's happening with your writing. You might set aside a day a week to work on a book." Another time he cautioned, "Don't neglect your tradition. You're a spiritual psychologist." After this I ended my fourteen-year hiatus from writing books. Thank you, Dallas and Jane (his wife), for how you've poured into us.

After Kristi and I started Soul Shepherding as a nonprofit ministry in 2009, our board kept affirming that God was having the greatest impact when people experienced not just one of us but *our relationship*. That's why Kristi joined me in writing this book. Thank you, John, Margaret, Betty, Ed, Jim, Joe, Steve, Joan, and Lance.

The content in this book was honed through many years of counseling ministry and by teaching it to pastors, church leaders, and others in our Soul Shepherding Institute and spiritual direction certificate training. Thank you to all the women and men who have shared their stories, hearts, and questions with us.

As you can see from the endnotes, numerous books have influenced us. There are four we'd like to make special mention of: *The Interior Castle* by Teresa of Ávila, *Stages of Faith* by James Fowler, *Mansions of the Heart* by our friend Tom Ashbrook, and *The Critical Journey* by Janet Hagberg and Robert Guelich. Thank you to these great writers.

When we started writing this manuscript, we kept hitting The Wall. Publishers said no, agents said no, manuscripts got thrown out, and we got more and more discouraged. Then we talked with our longtime mentors and friends, Dave and Jan Stoop (doctors of psychology like us), who encouraged us and connected us with our editor and publisher. Thank you, Dave and Jan.

A crucial part of the story was putting together our Soul Shepherding staff. After nearly ten years of trying *not* to grow an organization, we finally accepted it was God's call for us to lead a larger operation and minister on a larger stage. Our team helped us to manage and grow our ministry while writing this book. Thank you, Rob, Gina, Sue, Colleen, Shane, Miriam, Briana, and Historic Agency. Special thanks to Briana Gaultiere for creating the diagrams and illustrations in this book.

The next step was connecting with Don Gates, our literary agent. He gave us coaching, marketing, and connections we needed. Thank you, Don.

We finally broke through The Wall when Don reconnected us to our editor, Vicki Crumpton, and to Revell, a division of Baker Publishing Group. (Dave and Jan had initially connected us with Vicki, but it took a second try to get a green light from the committee.) She has been a godsend—delightful, affirming, and brilliant. The staff at Revell is top-notch and enthusiastic. Thank you, Vicki, Amy, Eileen, Abby, and the rest of the Revell team.

CHRIST Stages

- **Confidence in Christ (the C Stage)**
  Following Jesus Christ begins with receiving his forgiveness and new life.

- **Help in Discipleship (the H Stage)**
  We grow in community with Christ-followers and by practicing spiritual disciplines.

- **Responsibilities in Ministry (the R Stage)**
  We grow when we use our gifts to serve God and bless people.

- **The Wall (Transition)**
  Spiritual dryness or getting stuck is a hidden opportunity for deeper growth and joy.

- **Inner Journey (the I Stage)**
  We experience spiritual renewal through empathy, emotional growth, and longing for God.

- **Spirit-Led Ministry (the S Stage)**
  Our greatest joy and impact is to act with the presence and power of the Spirit to serve others.

- **Transforming Union (the T Stage)**
  Our journey of the soul culminates with being united in the generous love of Jesus Christ.

Introduction

A few years ago, I (Bill) hiked the Tunnel Trail in Santa Barbara, California, with my son David. It's a super-steep and strenuous trail up and down a quick succession of three 4,000-foot mountain peaks. At times the trail disappeared. In fact, we were warned that people had gotten lost there—*even the search and rescue team.* But those challenges made it a more exciting adventure!

We had been enjoying the hike, the sights, and our conversation when suddenly David stopped in his tracks. I bumped into him as he yelled, "Rattlesnake!" Right beside the trail ahead and hiding under a bush was a big rattler. It rattled its tail loudly, and its head was poised to strike. We bushwhacked on the other side of the trail to get around it.

Later we were hiking along and again David stopped. "This isn't the right trail," he announced. "We need to go back. You sure have to keep your wits about you on this trail." I replied, "Actually, I need to have *your* wits about me!" (He's an Eagle Scout.) The path of life is like that—we need a guide to know where we're going and to stay encouraged.

We all want to thrive in our life with Jesus, the Good Shepherd, but sometimes we can miss his path or get stuck in a dark valley.

God seems far away, Bible reading feels dry, prayer feels like going through lists, church becomes boring, or the activities that used to nourish us have stopped working. To make matters worse, typical approaches to spiritual growth that focus only on beliefs and behavior don't lead to lasting change. You're more than a "brain on a stick"[1] or a human-doing—you're a *soul on a journey with Jesus*. Your whole person needs to be shepherded with empathy and wisdom that's tailored for you.

Drawing from decades of study and over seventy thousand hours of providing therapy and spiritual direction, my wife, Kristi, and I have developed the CHRIST stages of faith. This model offers you a map of your soul that says, "You are here!" We help you identify which of the six stages you're currently experiencing or whether you're at The Wall. Then we guide you along a proven path of following Jesus to grow in emotional and spiritual health. We do this through our unique mapping tool, examples of people on the journey, insights on each stage, and suggested steps to grow within your stage.

Growing in the lessons and opportunities of your current stage prepares you for the next stage. It's an adventure of discovery in which you gain language for your struggles, needs, and opportunities. Since a community of believers often has people in each phase of the journey, it's vital to understand these stages of faith to enhance our empathy and acceptance of one another. Best of all, we provide customized recommendations to guide you in each stage with Scriptures, soul care practices, and spiritual disciplines. Furthermore, our small group leader guide and free videos help you and your friends apply the book material together.[2]

The CHRIST stages model is the lighted path of life for following Jesus that you and your friends have always needed. We've been teaching it since 2013 in our Soul Shepherding Institute. All kinds of Christ-followers and leaders have found these stages of faith to provide the framework for a powerfully transforming program of emotional and spiritual growth in the image of Christ.

"Bill, it's pouring rain and the weather report shows no signs of the storm letting up," Dallas Willard said to me on the phone one January day. "Jane is afraid for you to drive on the freeways."

"I'll be careful," I replied. "I'd still like to come talk with you— unless you need to reschedule."

"I'll be here in my office, and I'd much rather talk with you than keep digging through my stack of papers."

After two hours of dog-paddling on congested freeways, I was running and splashing through puddles on the University of Southern California campus. I had my Psalms prayer book carefully pressed against my chest, underneath my raincoat. In those days, I was carrying it everywhere in imitation of the Anonymous Pilgrim of the nineteenth century who walked barefoot through the Russian countryside praying the Jesus Prayer and blessing everyone he met.[3] I looked up into the rain and smiled at the statue of Dallas' mentor, John Wesley, offering a blessing.

Just ahead was the nearly one-hundred-year-old Mudd Hall of Philosophy building, modeled after an Italian monastery. It has a tall clock tower that chimes, statues of philosophers, gargoyles, and a cloistered walkway to a courtyard with a fountain. Ducking inside and out of the rain, I felt cozy. The hard tile floors in the hallway echoed with my footsteps, reminding me of the many times I'd waited outside Dallas' office, surrounded by thousands of books, and heard his footsteps approaching and keeping time as he cheerfully hummed a hymn.

But on this stormy evening he was waiting for me, relaxing in his side chair. As I sat down, he noticed my prayer book and asked to look at it. It was worn out from use, marked up on every page, stuffed full of little papers with my meditations and prayers, and held together by binder rings. He held it gently and slowly thumbed through it. "I see you've been nourishing yourself. The Psalms are the Bible's soul book. Wherever you turn, the passages leap off the page and get hold of your heart to help you ascend to God."

Dallas' spirit seemed to soar with the first verse of Psalm 23: "The Lord is my shepherd, I have life without lack." *Life without lack?* You might question that. *My life is full of lack—lack of resources, lack of health, lack of justice, lack of opportunity, lack of harmony in my relationships, lack of peace. Is the psalmist living in the real world? Is this life without lack just a fantasy?*

Dallas wrote, "[The Psalmist] is living in *the most real world*, a world where Yahweh is present and available and actively involved in the lives of those who know and trust him."[4] We talked about how the Twenty-third Psalm is a model for our journey of growing in God's grace. He encouraged me, "Psalm 23 covers the whole of the spiritual life in God's kingdom." Best of all, he smiled and said, "When you pray Psalm 23 you find that *Someone* is there waiting for you, to greet you and guide you."

That's why Dallas soaked his soul in this prayer song most every morning before he arose from bed. He wrote that it provides an "intensive internalization of the kingdom" and establishes "good epidermal responses of thought, feeling, and action" to integrate us "into the flow of God's eternal reign."[5]

We became quiet as we listened to the pouring rain. I felt as if we were huddled by a fire with Jesus on this cold, stormy night. I felt the warmth of our Shepherd's glowing face of love.

In those moments all the blessings God had brought me from praying the Shepherd Psalm over my lifetime seemed to come flooding back: calming my anxiety, discerning God's will, comforting a woman with terminal cancer, ministering healing to a woman with a migraine headache, teaching it to our children and watching how it helped them in their daily lives, and sharing its phases of growth with therapy clients and students.

In the journey ahead we'll draw on Psalm 23's progression of renewing metaphors and insights to highlight the CHRIST stages of emotional and spiritual growth. You'll enjoy green pastures of grace and be guided in the Shepherd's good path. You'll find comfort and encouragement in the dark valley. You'll receive a new anointing of the Spirit for how you can serve God. In the end your soul will sing with David, "My cup overflows. . . . I will dwell in the house of the LORD forever" (vv. 5–6).

As we travel, we'll enjoy growing intimacy with Jesus, and through him, the Trinity. Our soul comes *fully alive* as we love God, one another, and all people within our reach. Like Mary Magdalene at the empty tomb, we meet Christ risen when we hear him speak our name tenderly (John 20:11–18). Like Brother Lawrence, we learn to practice God's presence in all that we do.

***

Dear Jesus, our Good Shepherd, as we read, we pray that you personalize your path of life for each of us. Guide us in the stages of faith so we learn to grow in God's love, joy, peace, and power. Amen.

1

Shepherding Your Soul

To thrive in your life with Jesus
you need soul care and guidance.

Jesus says, "I am the good shepherd;
I know my sheep and my sheep know me."
John 10:14

"Y ou might as well divorce me and hire someone to cook and clean!" I (Kristi) screamed at Bill.

"Don't you ever use that word again!" he yelled back, and then he picked up his keys and drove away. In the hours he was gone, my rage melted into fear that he wouldn't come back and I'd be on my own with two little children.

I felt horrible for using the D word, but I was fed up with Bill's workaholism as a psychologist, pastor, and author. God had gifted and anointed him, but I needed more of his time and energy at home. I felt overwhelmed caring for our children and longed for more intimacy in our marriage. As long as I kept my desires buried, we got along great, but eventually my hurt and anger would erupt. Then he'd get defensive or angry, and I'd feel more hurt. Later he'd always apologize, empathize, and try to be more emotionally engaged for me and the kids. But the cycle kept repeating.

A few weeks later I (Bill) was in my home office writing a proposal to publish my fourth book, but my screen was blank. There was no tapping on the keys. But there was tapping on the door. "Daddy, can you play?" I saw my three-year-old son's big brown eyes peering at me through the glass doors. He smiled as he held up two Hot Wheels cars.

"I'm sorry, David. Daddy has to work today."

"But I wanna play cars, Daddy."

"I can't now, but we can play tonight." I put my head down, hiding behind my computer screen. I heard him start to cry and peeked over the top of my screen to see tears rolling down his chubby cheeks. Suddenly, Kristi swooped in with our one-year-old daughter, Jennie, in her arm and took hold of David's hand. She glared at me. I ducked back behind my screen. I didn't write any good words that day.

Not long after this, Kristi and I had a date night, and she tried a different tack to get my attention. Wooing, pleading, crying, and getting angry hadn't pulled me out of my workaholism. This time she gave me a handwritten card that asked, "Will you coauthor with me the lives of our *three* children?"

I exclaimed, "You're pregnant!" and gave her a big hug. That was a happy evening.

But her request to *coauthor* the lives of our children kept convicting my heart. Then a few days later I heard God's still, small voice whisper, "Will you take your dream of being a bestselling Christian author and lay it down on the altar? Will you do this out of love for me, Kristi, and your children?" I knew this heavenly voice, so I promised, "Yes, Lord, I will never write another book unless you tell me to."

Although I believed God's purpose was good, in the months to come I became confused and depressed. I kept asking, "Lord, why don't you want me to serve you with my writing? You gave me this gift—why are you taking it away? Why can't you help me love my family well *and* write books?"

I wanted to write books that cultivated intimacy with Jesus and wholeness of life for readers in the way that A. W. Tozer's *The Pursuit of God* had done for me as a young adult. Year after year I waited. I wished my situation was like Richard Foster's. When he obeyed the call of the Lord to give up his dream of writing *Celebration of Discipline*, God gave it back to him three days later.[1] As it turned out, my sacrifice lasted *fourteen years*. I felt like God didn't trust me. I felt lost and stuck because I didn't know about the stages of faith.

Have you ever felt like God didn't support your dream? Have you ever been confused or discouraged about your spiritual journey?

Downward Mobility

During my long season in a spiritual desert, the Lord provided Henri Nouwen as a wounded healer for me. I had heard the famous author and professor of Christian spirituality and psychology preach and had read some of his books. I was shocked that he chose to move from Harvard to L'Arche, from teaching the world's best and brightest students ready to rule the world to serving in a community for the mentally handicapped who had few words and seemingly no influence. Why would he trade his podium and microphone for a sponge and a bucket of soapy water? He decided to go *down* in his career. I had been trying to go *up*.

In his little book *In the Name of Jesus*, Nouwen confesses that *his success was endangering his soul*. Even though everyone was telling him he was doing good, inside he was lonely and his prayer life was empty. At first the spiritual death of leaving his prominent ministry post left him feeling depressed, worthless, and naked, with nothing to offer but his vulnerable self. But then he found community with the mentally handicapped and the freedom to be his true self.

He relished the fact that these people didn't read his books or care about his theological acumen. Instead of leading, he was being led. He explains, "They teach me about joy and peace, love and care and prayer—what I could never have learned in any academy. . . . They give me a glimpse of God's first love."[2] He met Jesus anew on the path of hiddenness and "downward mobility."[3] He became a caregiver offering meals, baths, and walks in the garden. He preached simple messages that children could understand. He discovered the power of smiling, remembering someone's name, and giving a hug.

Nouwen gave me words for my own emotional distress. (Years later, I realized he was describing what we call the Inner Journey or the I Stage of the CHRIST stages of faith and growth.) I had obeyed the Lord by no longer writing books, doing media appearances, or speaking in front of crowds of people. I was "just" a therapist and pastor of a counseling ministry. I felt like I was a nobody, going nowhere, and falling into nothingness. I shared my feelings with a counselor, with Kristi, and with soul friends. I received empathy, prayer, and affirmation for my true self, apart from my performances. I came to appreciate that the Lord was shepherding my personality and faith. I discovered the value of practicing the Little Way of Jesus by loving my family, clients, students, and other neighbors with simple kindnesses, openhearted listening, secret prayers, and life-on-life discipleship.[4] Over some years, I came to value this as more beneficial than public works for God with fanfare.

My sacrifice at the altar no longer felt like a loss. More than ever before, I was enjoying a new closeness with Christ, date nights and soul talks with Kristi, playing with my kids, and life as an *ordinary human being in God's world* that I wouldn't trade for anything. Furthermore, out of the blue one day I sensed the Spirit whisper, "Your pen will be your pulpit." Then I heard, "Take your pen off the altar and write. Look, your words are on fire!"

What a surprise! I was so happy the Lord called me to write again. That's when email was just becoming widely used, so I began sending out soul care messages to people. Instead of being a guru writing books for masses of people who needed my wisdom, I was a shepherd of souls writing devotionals for people who needed *Jesus*. Our Lord said, "Freely you have received; freely give" (Matt. 10:8). In just a few years, that turned into one million page views a year at SoulShepherding.org, with Kristi and me leading a growing ministry to pastors and others.

Your Journey of the Soul

Healthy faith engages our soul on a path of following Christ Jesus through six stages of emotional and spiritual development. To explore these stages, we'll draw on many Scripture passages and teachers of psychology and spirituality, including Teresa of Jesus. This sixteenth-century spiritual mother and classic devotional author from Ávila, Spain, pictures our soul as a beautiful and expansive interior castle. We follow "His Majesty" on an adventure through different "mansions" or stages of prayer and reflection. Little by little our Lord makes us "pure and full of all that is good," and our soul becomes increasingly "spacious, ample, and lofty."[5]

Notice that your soul isn't a wispy little ghost inside you that floats up to heaven when you die, like it's portrayed in movies. It's actually your whole person. Flowing out from deep inside you, it encompasses your body and expands out into your social world. In other words, your soul is so large that your body is actually inside your soul. That's why people in the same room can feel each other's energy and mood, even without talking.

Jesus our Shepherd leads us to drink from waters that nourish and strengthen our soul (Ps. 23:2–3). The still waters of Psalm 23 are "Eden spring water" (Ps. 36:8 MSG), the streams that make us glad (Ps. 46:4), the life-giving waters of Jesus' Spirit flowing into us and out from our belly to bless other people (John 7:37–39 KJV). Your soul, well cared for by God, invigorates and integrates all the functions of your being—emotions, thoughts, intentions, body, and relationships—into a flow of joyful, abundant, powerful, divine, and eternal life expressed in your unique personality.[6]

The story of the Anonymous Pilgrim of nineteenth-century Russia illustrates the journey of the soul. He was crippled, orphaned, homeless, and had nothing except his father's old Bible and a dream that he could learn to pray continually (1 Thess. 5:17). He found a *staretz* (spiritual director) who taught him to breathe a prayer thousands of times every day, just like the Desert Fathers and Mothers of the third and fourth centuries: *Lord Jesus Christ, have mercy on me, a sinner* (Luke 18:13, 38). The Jesus Prayer was sweet on his lips and in his heart as he walked barefoot from village to village, begging for bread in exchange for whatever work he could do. On his pilgrimage the Lord transformed him from being a depressed recluse to a joyful disciple of Christ who brought salvation to the lost, healing to the sick, love to his enemies, and intimacy with God to untold millions of people.[7]

A Map for Your Journey

A backpacker told me (Bill) that when he was weary on a remote stretch of the Pacific Crest Trail he encountered "trail angels" who showed up out of nowhere with water, food, medicine, encouragement, and a map. This reminded me of when our son David was eleven years old and I took him on a twelve-mile hike up Saddleback Mountain near our home in Orange County, California. It was a wonderful father-and-son adventure—till we headed down and got lost on the backside of the mountain. We were alone, with no map and no cell service. We'd eaten all our food and it was getting dark and cold. We were scared and I was beating myself up about not being better prepared. But I kept praying to God for help. About an hour later, we heard the voices of two hikers who had a map and guided us down the mountain!

At times we all need a map with a big red star that says "You are here!" In this book Kristi and I offer you a map of your journey with personalized guidance on the way of Jesus.[8] We expand on the Bible's brief outline of three stages of faith: "dear children," "young people," and spiritual "fathers and mothers" (1 John 2:12–14 TPT).[9] Based on extensive research[10] and field-testing, our model for the CHRIST stages of faith emphasizes following Jesus in a journey of increasing emotional and spiritual health:

- **Confidence in Christ (the C Stage)**
  By receiving God's Spirit we are born from above to begin the great adventure of following Jesus Christ!

- **Help in Discipleship (the H Stage)**
  We grow in God's grace through community with other Christians and practicing spiritual disciplines like participating in church services and Bible studies.

- **Responsibilities in Ministry (the R Stage)**
  It's an honor to use our gifts to serve God and others in our church, family, community, or job, but we're prone to get in trouble from being overly ambitious or relying on ourselves rather than the Spirit of God.

- **Through The Wall (Transition)**
  Due to overworking, spiritual dryness, a faith crisis, or suffering, we may find ourselves at The Wall. Usually this happens in the R Stage and is worked through in the I Stage, but at each stage we face a roadblock that may become The Wall.

- **Inner Journey (the I Stage)**
  Getting stopped at The Wall evokes emotional distress. If we take courage to share our emotions, struggles, and sins with safe people and in prayer, then we come into a new intimacy with Jesus and Abba.

- **Spirit-Led Ministry (the S Stage)**
  Now we learn a new way of serving—not by working *for* God in our own strength, but by working *with* God in

Jesus' easy yoke. We enjoy overflowing with God's grace to others.

- **Transforming Union (the T Stage)**
  Our life and work become increasingly about practicing the presence of the Trinity in all we do. Joyfully united with Christ, we are more able to love all people, even our enemies.

The CHRIST Stages Map

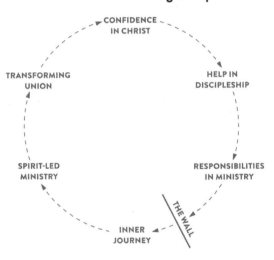

Your progression through the CHRIST stages (or phases) of faith is not linear but circular. Try picturing this map like a 3D spiral, because emotional and spiritual growth in God's grace is an up-and-down journey in which we go back and forth between developmental phases. At any time we may revisit a previous phase for deeper learning or remain in one phase for many years. As we'll discuss later, many Christ-followers become stuck and do not grow beyond the early stages. Our opportunity is to grow in God's grace at each stage. Even if we experience the T Stage, that is not a destination but a doorway to return to the C Stage and the other stages, whether for personal needs or to offer empathy and encouragement for others. The CHRIST stages map shows the general path in our journey of increasing union with our Lord.

Your Map Key

I (Kristi) wish I had this map twenty years ago when I was an insecure and overwhelmed young woman who secretly judged and hated her emotional self. I was preoccupied trying to prove my worthiness through good works and service. The map shows me that I had come to The Wall in the stage of Responsibilities in Ministry and was unwittingly resisting the Inner Journey. It helps me to realize that through accepting and expressing my emotions to God and my friends and setting my heart's desire on the Lord, I could eventually get through The Wall. This model has provided great insight on how I can experience more intimacy, meaning, and power in my life with Christ.

In Bill's case, this CHRIST stages map would've helped him to understand that, when he got depressed after surrendering his dream, he wasn't being judged by God—it was the father of lies attacking him (John 8:44; Rev. 12:10). The map shines a light on Bill's dark season of spiritual dryness and discouragement at The Wall and helps him see the Spirit of Jesus drawing him into the Inner Journey. This opens him to the blessing of the Lord befriending his emotions and inflaming his heart with love.

Chapter by chapter we'll unveil your personal map to help you locate yourself on the journey through the CHRIST stages. Identifying your current stage will help you to receive God's grace at your point of need and take the next steps that will most help you to grow. At each stage we suggest particular Scriptures, prayers, and devotional activities that will further your growth in emotional and spiritual health. We've also suggested contemporary Christian worship songs to fit each stage and created small group curriculum and other resources to go with this book.[11]

To help you understand your journey ahead you'll want to remember these key terms:

- **Soul** refers to your whole, embodied person. When healthy, your soul integrates all the dynamics of your personality (thoughts, emotions, will, body, and relationships) to flow with divine life and love.
- **CHRIST stages of faith** are six developmental phases[12] of emotional and spiritual growth. Each stage builds on the one before and prepares you for the one after. Often we revisit earlier stages.
- **Home stage** refers to your primary CHRIST stage of faith. Since growth is a spiral, you may relate to more than one stage. But it's hard to understand people two stages beyond you, and you may have conflict with them.
- **Roadblocks to grace** are trials at each stage that may become The Wall and tempt us to turn back to the previous stage. The major roadblock is The Wall in the middle.
- **First Half** and **Second Half** refer to the three CHRIST stages on either side of The Wall. The two halves present different faith orientations and spiritualities that are in tension.
- **Grace** is God's favor and power offered to you through Christ to help you grow in emotional and spiritual health at each stage of faith. Grace is unhurried, so it's important to take the time you need in each stage.
- **Faith** is responding to God's grace with trust and confidence so that you love God, others, and yourself more and more.
- **Spiritual disciplines** are bodily activities to develop habits to rely on Jesus, care for your soul, and love God and people well. Certain disciplines work best at each stage, but often you can benefit from the ones in previous stages.

Becoming Like Jesus

Throughout this book we'll be looking at people in the Bible, church history, and contemporary life growing in emotional and spiritual health through the stages of faith. Most of all, we'll look at Jesus Christ as our model. That's why we call them *CHRIST* stages. Henri Nouwen put it well: "There is no journey to God outside of the journey that Jesus made."[13] Our Lord has gone before us on the path of life, and he shows us the way to love God and neighbor. To trace the steps of our Master, let's turn to the Gospel of Luke, which puts special emphasis on the Son of God's personal development as a human being who is our Living Blueprint.[14]

Jesus showed **Confidence in God** (C Stage) at an early age. He developed a loving relationship with his Father in heaven through people who cared for him, especially his mother, who treasured him and pondered his significance (2:19, 51). As a boy in **Help in Discipleship** (H Stage), our Lord grew in strength, wisdom, and favor with God and people. His parents and others (like the synagogue leaders in Nazareth) helped him learn to worship God, read the Scriptures, pray, and serve others (2:40–52). As a young adult Jesus grew in **Responsibilities in Ministry** (R Stage) through teaching the Scriptures (2:42–47) and loving people in his job as a carpenter (4:22). During these hidden years he may have encountered **The Wall**, doing manual labor for many years (3:23; 4:22), being rejected by his hometown (4:28–30), and being pressured by unfair expectations from his family (8:19–21). Yet through these trials he loved others with joy.

At the start of his public ministry when Jesus was thirty years old, he was renewed in the **Inner Journey** (I Stage). First he was baptized by John in the Jordan River and had a special experience of grace in which he heard his Father's voice from heaven proclaim, "You are my Son, whom I love; with you I am well pleased" (3:22). Then the Spirit drew him into the desert wilderness for forty days, and this included testing from Satan at **The Wall** and more **Inner**

Journey growth through solitude, fasting, Scripture meditation, and prayer to foster intimacy with his Father, clarify his ministry calling, and resist Satan by resolving to do God's will (4:1–13). Even during his busy ministry Jesus often withdrew to be alone with his Abba, which was the source of his compassion, wisdom, and power (5:16; 6:12).

In much of Luke's Gospel, we see Jesus in **Spirit-Led Ministry** (S Stage). He teaches people from God's Word with the confident authority of having personally lived it out (4:32). He listens for and follows his Father's directions for ministry (4:42–44; 6:12–13). He heals the sick (4:31–5:26; 8:26–56), feeds the hungry (9:10–17), and drives out demons by the finger of God (11:20). He delegates ministry to his disciples so that they can carry on his work (10:1). Out of the overflow of his prayer life he teaches them to pray (11:1–13).

In the second half of his Gospel, Luke shows our Master in **Transforming Union** (T Stage). Jesus is revealed as the Messiah of God (9:18–27). He shows how completely he is united with God when he glows with light and glory on the Mount of Transfiguration (9:28–36). He embodies God's love for the disadvantaged: ethnic minorities (10:25–37), women (10:38–42), lepers (17:11–19), widows (18:1–8), little children (18:15–17), beggars (18:35–43), and tax collectors (19:1–10). For all people he unveils the beauty of his Father's world (12:22–34). Then on the journey of the cross he re-encounters **The Wall** and moves through it into the full flower of **Transforming Union** by forgiving those who abused him and blessing everyone in his reach (23:32–43). With his last breath he submits himself completely into his Father's hands to reconcile us to God (23:46). Then, by the power of the Spirit, Jesus rises from the dead and ascends into the heavens (24:1–53).

That's a human being *fully alive!* Jesus is full of God's fatherly love and exuberant with joy (10:21). Jesus is so radiantly winsome with divine life that thirty-two times Luke says crowds of people gathered around him to be close to him. Again and again people press through the throngs to touch *the Heavenly Man.* Four men cut a hole in a roof to drop their sick friend at Jesus' feet (5:17–20). A rejected woman forced into sex slavery breaks into a house full of religious men, falls at Jesus' feet weeping, and pours out her alabaster jar of expensive ointment on his feet (7:36–50). A sick woman crawls in the dirt between people's legs to touch the hem of his garment (8:42–48). Zacchaeus climbs a tree to get above the parade of people so he can see Jesus, and then he jumps down to have dinner with him (19:1–10).

Jesus Christ is captivating! To follow him in a journey of increasing grace is the best life we could hope for.

Soul Care Practice

Praying Psalm 23

I (Kristi) remember when our son David was about eighteen months old. He watched Bill go to work with his lunch box and decided he wanted one too. He put some special things in a little box: a package of raisins, his favorite Matchbox car, a piece of his blankie, and his pacifier. He was trying to be like his daddy! We smiled as our little boy carried his Special Things Box around the house with such pride and happiness. He was ready to face the world.

His box contained more than nice little play things—as psychologists we call them "transitional objects" because they help children *transition* from feeling secure with Mommy to feeling secure even when she's not in sight.[15] For instance, David associated his pacifier and blankie with the comfort of being nursed by his mommy. His little treasures gave him inner strength and contentment when he played alone or went to bed at night.

It's good to put Psalm 23 in your Soul Kit. When the COVID-19 pandemic brought anxiety, fear, and grief, we pulled it out to rest in our Shepherd's love. For decades we've used it in our teaching and small groups as a resource for God's peace and guidance. Neurological research shows how transformational a spiritual discipline like this can be. The brain scans of people who practiced attentive and focused prayer twelve minutes a day for eight weeks showed significant improvement in the areas of their brains that support social interaction, compassion, stress reduction, low blood pressure, resistance to irrational urges, and peace.[16]

Psalm 23 Meditation

Let's saturate our souls in Psalm 23 now. As you'll discover, it's a developmental journey that parallels the CHRIST stages. It's helpful to find a quiet place and get comfortable. Pray with me:

The Lord is my shepherd, I shall not want.

Jesus proclaims, "I am the Good Shepherd" (John 10:11). At the beginning of our journey we come to know Jesus as our Savior and Life-Giver. We put our confidence in the Lord who meets our needs.

He makes me lie down in green pastures.

Imagine yourself with the sheep in a lush, green pasture. Keep grazing on God's grace till you're full! Then let yourself lie down in that green grass. Feel its softness; feel your body relax and lighten.

Jesus is our Bread of Life. He fills our hungry souls, so we can rest in him, find our contentment in him, and grow in trust and peace.

He leads me beside the still waters.

Why still waters? Because sheep are afraid of the rushing waters and can't get a drink. Jesus says, "Are you thirsty? Come to me . . . A spring of living water will gush up into a flowing stream . . . You will never be thirsty again! I offer *living waters*. I will give you fresh, pure water that satisfies your thirst."[17] Drink in the Spirit and be refreshed.

He restores my soul.

In the still waters we can also be baptized, immersed in God's love. Imagine it's a hot day and you wade into the cool water to be cleansed and revitalized . . . When you get out of the water, the ripples fade, and the pool is like smooth glass . . . Now look into the water and see Good Shepherd with you, his reflection and yours together. See his smile? You're totally forgiven, loved, and made new!

He leads me down the path of righteousness for his name's sake.

Sheep are prone to wander and get lost. They follow other sheep and may get stuck in pricker bushes. But Jesus knows the best way and he leads us. Maybe you're at a fork in the road with a decision to make. Maybe you're struggling to love someone well. Ask Christ to guide you.

Even though I walk through the valley of the shadow of death, I will fear no evil, for you are with me.

There are seasons when Good Shepherd needs to lead us through the dark valley, past snakes and cougars. Of course, we don't want to go this way, but it's the route to the high country where the temperatures are cool and the grass is green during the hot summer months.

Jesus promises, "Never will I leave you; never will I forsake you . . . I am with you always, even to the end of the age . . . So fear not, little flock of sheep, it is your Father's good pleasure to give you his kingdom."[18]

Your rod and your staff comfort me.

Our Savior uses his rod to fight off our enemies. If we wander from the fold, he flings it out just beyond us to startle us and call us back into safe boundaries. He uses his staff to guide his sheep and to free us when we slip into a ravine. At night he uses his staff to have his sheep pass under it, so he can separate our wool to see if any parasites or prickers need to be taken out.

Let's thank Jesus for how he shepherds us through our trials and troubling emotions and gives us courage.

You prepare a table before me in the presence of my enemies.

Our Shepherd provides an abundant feast for us! We sit at the table and eat because the Lord is with us; it's a place of community and celebration—even with enemies around us. It's at the table that Jesus Christ breaks bread and pours wine, gives his body and blood to forgive us and heal our sins, to reconcile us to God. As the Lord forgives us, then we can forgive those who mistreat us and be at peace (Col. 3:13).

You anoint my head with oil. My cup overflows.

Shepherd Jesus heals our wounds with his special oil. He anoints us for ministry as wounded healers who understand and have compassion for others who are hurting or struggling.

Jesus is so good to us! God's unconditional love is spilling out and splashing onto us! Pray for it to *overflow* from you to others.

Surely goodness and mercy shall follow me all the days of my life.

At the beginning of this journey we were like children and Good Shepherd was like a directive parent: he *made* us to lie down in his green pastures and he *led* us to walk his path of righteousness. Then, in the middle of our journey, we found ourselves in a dark valley trial. We felt as if the Lord had left us alone. But then we realized that he was *with* us, right beside us all along in our hard times.

Now, as we near the end of our journey, goodness and mercy *follow* us. The Spirit of Jesus is letting us be a step ahead because we're growing up and we've learned the path in our heart. Still, at times we need our Shepherd to whisper from behind, "This is the way; walk in it" (Isa. 30:21).

And I will dwell in the house of the Lord forever.

With the psalmist we pray, "Blessed are those who dwell in your house, O Lord. I would rather be a doorkeeper in the house of my

God than dwell in the tents of the wicked" (Ps. 84:4, 10). We're learning to appreciate our intimacy and union with the Father and Son as we go about our life. In every part of the journey the loving Spirit is before us, beside us, and behind us. Amen.[19]

Soul Talk

1. What are your thoughts about life being a journey with Jesus that goes through stages of emotional and spiritual growth?

2. How do you relate to Bill's or Kristi's story? Or to Henri Nouwen's downward mobility?

3. What especially interests you about the journey of emotional and spiritual growth in the CHRIST stages of faith?

4. What is something you appreciated about Jesus' own journey through the CHRIST stages?

5. What did you appreciate about the meditation on Psalm 23?

2

Grace for Your Journey

You grow by relying on God's favor and power in the ups and downs of life.

Jesus says, "I am the gate for the sheep."

John 10:7

When I (Kristi) met Laura,[1] she was in her late forties. She was a highly paid business executive and church leader. She hung her head and began to share:

I don't know what's wrong with me. I have a great life, a great family, and a great job, but I'm not happy. I've gained fifteen pounds and I can't make myself exercise. I lie awake in the night and am exhausted all day—caffeine doesn't even bring me energy. I'm trying to get my act together, so I'm seeing a functional medicine doctor, and my daughter, husband, and I are on the Whole30 elimination diet.

I'm under so much pressure at work because if I can't meet payroll this week it will hurt my employees. I feel responsible to God for them. I used to enjoy my work and feel like God was pleased with me, but now I'm so stressed out. My daughter says I'm not fun to be with anymore, and my husband and I aren't really connecting except to watch TV or go shopping.

The worst thing is I've lost any sense of God's presence—even church feels like a burden and a duty. I keep serving because I'm needed, but I find myself leaving church with more questions than answers. I used to be so confident in God's love. I even encouraged other people's faith, but now God feels distant and I'm filled with doubts.

Cycling in Works or Grace

Laura was a longtime Bible student, yet under the surface of her theology there was an unconscious self-reliance embedded into her habits. Despite her grace-based theology, her operating mode in her work and family was to rely more on her own abilities and resources rather than on the Spirit of life and peace (Rom. 8:6–8). Internally she had a hidden legalist directing her life, so she got stuck in the Cycle of Works. Her journey through the CHRIST stages stalled because she was pressured, ego-oriented, emotionally shut down, distant from God, tired, and empty (see the figure below).

Cycle of Works

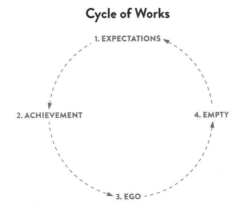

1. EXPECTATIONS

2. ACHIEVEMENT

3. EGO

4. EMPTY

The Cycle of Works goes counterclockwise. We start with the unconscious emotional belief that we need to measure up to certain *conditions* to feel acceptable or for God to be pleased with us. So the pressure is on for *achievement* in our work, family, church, physical appearance, social media, or whatever we're into. Spiritually, we live by shoulds: *Read the Bible every day . . . Don't miss church . . . Be kind to everyone . . . Help those in need . . .* We judge ourselves (or others) for not measuring up. We're trying to build up our *ego* in other people's eyes (and our own) based on our performance. We're trying to stay in control and not be vulnerable, but this posture of self-reliant pride and earning leaves us tired and *empty*. We may get resentful toward God: *I'm doing all these things for you, Lord, and what am I getting out of it?* We may try to cope with the hole in our soul by turning to media, sinful temptations, or addictive behavior. We're likely to struggle with anxiety, depression, unhealthy relationships, and feeling distant from God.

God's alternative is the Cycle of Grace[2] (see below), which fuels our emotional and spiritual growth in the CHRIST stages of faith. It goes clockwise in the opposite direction of the Cycle of Works. It starts with Jesus showing us God's *acceptance*. Experiencing unconditional love and becoming securely attached to Christ Jesus and the Father gives us *energy*. Now our motivation for what we do

Cycle of Grace

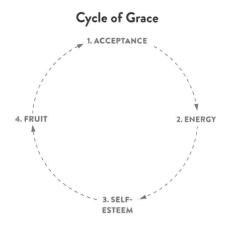

4. FRUIT

1. ACCEPTANCE

2. ENERGY

3. SELF-ESTEEM

comes from the Lord—not from trying to achieve or prove our value. This helps us to develop our *self-esteem*, so we become increasingly humble, confident, and stable. The outcome of grace is *fruit*: we're able to do effective work, and our life bears the fruit of the Spirit that blesses other people and honors God (Gal. 5:22–23). This is living in Jesus' easy yoke (Matt. 11:25–30).

There is also a Cycle of Pseudograce, which is increasingly common in our post-Christian culture. It substitutes *tolerance* or *self-acceptance* for God's grace, and its goal is so-called freedom— especially from standards of what is right and good—rather than the fruit of the Spirit. This Cycle of Pseudograce is really another version of the Cycle of Works that is self-generated and leaves us languishing in our journey with Jesus—largely empty of divine love, joy, peace, and power.

In Ephesians 2 Paul teaches the principles in the Cycle of Grace. First, God offers great love and rich mercy to us, accepting and esteeming us freely and fully, which motivates our apprenticeship to Christ (v. 4). Then, even though we were spiritually dead in sin (unresponsive to the Spirit of love), God made us energetically alive with Christ and raised us up with him to live in the heavenly realms (vv. 5–6). God recreates us to be a new self in Christ; *we are God's best work of art* (v. 10).[3] Grace culminates in the fruit of our good works of love, which God prepared in advance for us to do (v. 10).

Grace as Favor

In Paris, Bill and I viewed Monet's *Water Lily* paintings at the Musée de l'Orangerie. In one room huge panoramic murals of his garden pond in the four seasons encircled us. Tour groups studied artistic details of the paintings, moving from one room to the next, but we were enraptured for two hours as we sat and prayed. We got *inside* Monet's garden.

Grace is like that—it's not just a theological concept of "unmerited favor." When we think of grace only as either forgiveness or a transaction that happened at the cross, then we miss out on the joy of a friendly and empowering relationship with Jesus.

May the Holy Spirit help us to read the Bible in a way that we appreciate Christ in the text as the Sun of Righteousness rising with healing in his rays![4]

I (Bill) have read all thirteen of Brennan Manning's books, many of them more than once. Why? Because he keeps reminding me, "God loves you as you are and not as you should be!"[5] He assures me that the Abba of Jesus is very fond of me. I feel Jesus' *splagchnizomai* (splangkh-nid'-zom-ahee), which is Greek for "guts of compassion" and is "quite different from superficial and ephemeral emotions of pity or sympathy. [Jesus'] heart was torn, His gut wrenched, the most vulnerable part of His being laid bare."[6] Absorbing the unconditional grace and unfailing compassion of God through Jesus Christ takes away our guilt and shame. "It's like slipping into a tub of hot water and letting God's love wash over us and enfold us."[7] We feel clean, relaxed, refreshed, warm, and held. Absolutely *nothing* can separate us from the way God's unstoppable love embraces us in Jesus our Master![8]

We're also in danger of making the opposite mistake with grace by thinking it means *we don't need to do anything.* As Dallas Willard liked to say, "Grace is not opposed to effort, it is opposed to earning."[9] If we're not careful we can get *paralyzed by grace.*[10] In this case we misrepresent God's sovereignty and grace so that our free choice and personal responsibility are diminished. We tell ourselves it's all up to the omni-Lord who gets saved or healed or helped and how things work out in our world, so we feel no urgency to do the work of God's kingdom. We become stuck like a car on the side of the road with our hood up, waiting till the heavenly AAA comes to pick us up and take us to heaven. Actually, the Lord wants us to drive on down the road of life and to converse with him about where we go and what we do. Our relationship with God is meant to be a partnership.

Grace as Power

In 1926 Ira Yates had a profitable business storefront that he sold to buy a 26,000-acre sheep ranch in Texas. Sadly, there was a drought. All of his sheep and goats died, and he couldn't provide for his family. To survive they had to live on welfare and were about to lose their home and ranch. As a last-ditch attempt to survive, Ira asked his friend who worked for Transcontinental Oil to drill on his land to see if there was any oil. His friend wouldn't do it, insisting that his company and others had tried drilling all over that area and there was no oil. But Yates kept hounding him till finally one day they did come. They drilled for twenty-two days and came up empty. They were going to give up, but Yates convinced them to give it one more day, and that was the day they struck oil. It was a vast treasure trove of rich crude oil that gushed up and is still producing to this day.

Paul, the apostle of grace, helps us drill down into a hidden reservoir of riches sitting right under our feet. Paul uses the word "grace" over one hundred times in his writings—that's more than half of the times it's used in the Bible.[11] If you study these and other Scriptures on grace, you'll see that God's favor comes with power. Dallas Willard taught that as disciples of Jesus we're designed to burn grace like a jet plane burns fuel to lift off the ground and soar into the skies.[12] That's explosive energy! You know you're receiving God's grace when you respond to divine initiative by listening to the Holy Spirit, obeying Scripture, drawing on the Prince of Peace in a trial, or sharing mercy and compassion with people. In other words, grace inspires your faith and reliance on the activity of the risen Christ with you.

Look at the grace-power for growing spiritually and emotionally with Jesus in the Kingdom of the Heavens:[13]

- Jesus grew in God's grace and was *strengthened* in his personal development and relationships (Luke 2:40).
- The first Christ-followers grew rapidly as individuals and as a community because much grace with *great power* came upon them (Acts 4:33).
- Grace makes us *bold* to testify to people about the good news of Jesus (Acts 20:24).
- God graces us with special *gifts and abilities* (Rom. 12:6).
- God makes *all* grace abound to us so we have *all* we need in *all* things and at *all* times and we can abound in *all* good works (2 Cor. 9:8).
- Like Paul we can be joyful and thankful in trials and personal weaknesses because God's *power* sustains us (2 Cor. 12:8–10).
- Grace *energizes* us to do good works (Eph. 2:8–10).
- The great grace of God *empowers* us to say no to sin and yes to being godly (Titus 2:11–14).

One way I check myself to see if I'm tapping into the energy of God's lavish grace is to pay attention to how I react when I'm discouraged, stressed, or worn out. It's easy to turn to Instagram, TV, or snacking. It's good to relax, but vegging out or numbing will not care for our soul. Instead, if we touch base with Jesus by telling him how we feel or seeking empathy from a friend, we can tap into God's grace. Then we can scroll social media with a prayerful heart or give thanks for healthy and tasty food.

If we habitually turn to false comforts to veg out, it shows we're not absorbing God's grace-power into our soul-life and that our faith is weak and insecure. Unhealthy coping mechanisms are unconscious ego maneuvers that hijack our personality. We're denying our distress and our need to be governed by grace. We're trying to secure ourselves in this world rather than trusting God to nourish and strengthen us in the spiritual world of the kingdom of righteousness, peace, and joy in the Holy Spirit (Matt. 6:25–34; Rom. 14:17).

Peaks and Pits

When we were raising our three children, at dinner we shared our "peak" and our "pit" of the day. We all took turns to talk about our day and listen to one another with empathy, and then we prayed together. This type of soul talk helps us to appreciate that in the events of our day we're not left alone to manage our life in the Cycle of Works. Instead, like faltering Peter who learned to be "Petros the Rock," we can rely on *the God of all grace* to replenish and strengthen us to stand firm in the true grace and eternal glory that are ours in Christ Jesus (1 Pet. 5:10–12).

In your journey through the CHRIST stages of faith you'll experience lots of spiritual peaks and pits. Everyone's experience is unique, but generally mature disciples of Jesus are likely to experience (even reexperience) two high points separated by a valley (as depicted in the figure below). These movements are like the ocean tide rising and falling. Ignatius of Loyola, the sixteenth-century founder of the Jesuits, called these rhythms "consolations" and "desolations."[4] Surprisingly, *our lows as well as our highs are expressions of God's grace and are opportunities for learning.*

Consolation refers to times in which we feel the warmth of God's presence or the sense that we're blessed and encouraged by our

Consolations and Desolations Timeline

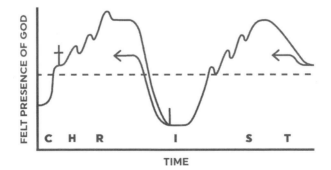

Lord. We get exciting new insights from the Bible, enjoy prayer, relax quietly in God's presence, experience intimacy with God in worship, have rich spiritual conversations, or feel our service is impactful. We need to resist Satan tempting us to take credit for these experiences of grace. Then the Lord can use these blessed interior movements to lead us into the next stage of deepening grace and fruitfulness.

In times of *desolation*, blessed feelings evaporate and God seems far away. Desolation is the psalmist crying out to Yahweh, "How long will you hide your face from me?" (13:1). We do the same spiritual activities as before, but now they don't bring satisfaction. We pray, but it seems that God does not answer. We go to church, but it's boring. We doubt doctrines we used to believe. In our spiritual life we feel restless, bored, distracted, discouraged, dry as dust. We lose motivation to seek God. Worst of all, in desolation, *here comes the judge* saying our faith is deficient, we've regressed spiritually, and it's our fault we can't feel God's presence. Then we put pressure on ourselves to do more and more spiritual activities.

In desolations, Satan tempts us to discouragement, resentment, and cynicism. Our opportunity is to keep trusting that *God truly loves us and is growing us in the CHRIST stages of faith even when we don't see it or feel it.*

Desolation is different from being depressed, although the two affect each other. Depression is a psychological problem that darkens our whole personality and life, including our relationship with God and spiritual activities. Desolation is a *spiritual experience* of feeling God's absence, which can affect our personal well-being. Depression is caused by negative thinking, unresolved grief, repressed anger, relationship problems, or a biochemical imbalance. Desolation is the Holy Spirit gently and persistently teaching us to trust that although our heavenly Father may be unfelt at the time, he loves us and wills good for us.

Furthermore, desolation is not the same as being disciplined by God for sin. When you're in desolation it's not because you did anything wrong. It's not because you lack faith. It's not something you can fix by doing more spiritual disciplines or spending more time at church. Rather, in desolation, the Lord is doing a deep and mysterious work of grace in us, withdrawing our *felt sense* of the Spirit's presence to reveal our hurts and needs in order to re-form us in love.

The apostle James teaches that in the arid desert of desolation there is surprising joy if we persevere in asking God for what we need, believing in the unseen Spirit's generosity, and valuing our opportunity to mature in godly character (1:2–6). He adds that to experience God's joy and health we may need to ask someone to receive our confession of sin and pray for us (5:13–16). Trusting God in desolation doesn't feel like growth. That's because grace is working inside our soul and may not improve our circumstances. Psychologically, we're learning to trust our unseen and unfelt Lord and internalize his Spirit so that out of sight is not out of mind.[15]

Bigger Hands

The key to growing in God's grace in the ups and downs of our journey of faith is relying not on our own abilities in the Cycle of Works but on "the Spirit of Jesus"[16] in the Cycle of Grace. Dallas Willard gave me a great example of this when I completed his two-week seminary class "Spirituality and Ministry," which was conducted as a monastery retreat. The first evening I wrote in my journal:

The first words that Dallas spoke this morning will undoubtedly prove to be the most important of this whole class. His comment shows me where our professor's heart is, that he's practicing his motto: "Do your best, but don't trust your best—trust God." He made an off-the-cuff remark, almost under his breath. His assistant had just concluded the introductory discussion of the course syllabus when he signed off, "That's enough from me. It's time

to turn the class over to bigger hands." Then Dallas quipped, "I
hope it's also in Someone's bigger hands."

You might think that's just Dallas' quick wit. Actually, it's something he'd prayed about:

> One of my great joys came when I got up from a chair to walk to
> the podium and the Lord said to me, "Now remember, it's what I
> do with the words between your lips and their hearts that matters."
> That is a tremendous lesson. If you do not trust God to do that,
> then he will let you do what you're going to do, and it's not going
> to come to much. But once you turn it loose and recognize we are
> always inadequate, but our inadequacy is not the issue, you are able
> to lay that burden down. Then the satisfaction you have in Christ
> spills over into everything you do.[17]

Dallas knew that his own abilities and works were not enough.
To excel as a teacher, be a good friend, or do anything well he
needed to enjoy and rely on the presence and power of the Spirit
of the risen Christ with him. I experienced this as I listened to him
teach, when I was with him at events, and when he took my hands to
pray for me after our meetings. Of the many lessons I have learned
from him, the most important is to do my best in whatever I do
and *put my confidence not in myself but in the God of all grace with me.*

"Why Am I Not Feeling God's Care?"

I (Kristi) gave Laura a quick overview of the CHRIST stages to
show her that she seemed to be in the R Stage of Responsibilities
in Ministry. She was excelling by using her gifts and working hard
in her job, home, and church. But she'd been overworking and
straining to achieve and boost her ego. Now she found herself at
The Wall in a spiritually dry season, trying to soldier on dutifully
in her work for God. She kept saying, "What's happening? Why am
I not feeling God's care for me anymore? What's wrong with me?"

Being in a soul season of desolation left Laura distrusting God's goodness and shaming herself; she was blocked from enjoying grace. But the CHRIST stages map highlighted that the Holy Spirit was calling her into the I Stage of the Inner Journey. It was time for her to set boundaries on overworking in the R Stage and make more soul space. Doing I-Stage practices like seeking empathy, praying with emotional honesty, abiding in Christ, and cultivating longing for God would help her enjoy the grace of a closer relationship with Jesus and his Father.

At each of the CHRIST stages there is a key conflict that we'll be unpacking in the chapters to come (see table below). On one side you'll face a roadblock in the form of a personal struggle, and on the other side you can find a new experience of God's abundant grace that can help you to grow in your identity in Christ. Often roadblocks feel like desolation and grace feels like consolation. In both trials and blessings, the Spirit ministers to us, and Satan tempts us. With support from Christ and people who build you up in faith and service, you can "become mature, attaining to the whole measure of the fullness of Christ" (Eph. 4:11–13). Appreciating and growing in the grace of each stage prepares you for the next stage of increasing intimacy with Jesus.

STAGE OF FAITH	ROADBLOCK	GRACE
Confidence in Christ	Soul splits	Sticky love
Help in Discipleship	Misinterpreting Scripture	God's Word in community
Responsibilities in Ministry	False identity	Joy gifts for serving God
The Wall (Transition)	Distrusting God	God's empathy
Inner Journey	Denial of emotions	Deeper experiences of God's love
Spirit-Led Ministry	Dark Night of the Soul	Surprise blessings to share
Transforming Union	Diminishing Jesus Christ	Practicing God's presence

As you'll see in the coming chapters, the CHRIST stages of emotional and spiritual growth are not separate boxes—they're overlapping phases, as the Holy Spirit leads us to spiral up and down the developmental progression. In grace and health each stage is like a teeter-totter in which we may move back and forth between our home stage and the stage before or after. But if we resist the Spirit of grace at our home stage, then we can get stuck. This is especially the case at The Wall, which is the transition between the R Stage and the I Stage that threatens to thwart our journey in God's expanding grace.

In Laura's case, her path to get unstuck was to make more space and energy for the Inner Journey, so I encouraged her to set better boundaries at her job and take a season off from her leadership responsibilities at church. She needed to get out of the rut of overworking to exhaustion and then checking out emotionally in entertainment. It was time for her to learn how to receive care for her soul and rest in God's embracing grace through being emotionally honest with a safe friend. She learned to engage Scripture with this same vulnerability and found it awakened her heart's desire for God.

Additionally, Laura benefited from spiritual biographies. For instance, she read a retelling of the Bible's story of John the Baptist's crisis of doubt and saw that even a great prophet like John suffered, felt far from God, and questioned whether Jesus truly was the Messiah (Matt. 11:2–6).[18] This validated her emotions and helped her not to feel alarmed and alone or to judge herself. It gave her language for her experience and a vision for how to get out of the deadly vortex of the Cycle of Works and into Jesus' life-giving Cycle of Grace.

To summarize, when you're stressed or spiritually dry, here are some steps you can take to experience the unfailing grace of God:

1. Identify your CHRIST stage and needs.
2. Set limits to make soul space.
3. Seek empathy through Scripture and friends.
4. Read spiritual biographies (see the soul care practice below).

Soul Care Practice

Reading Stories of Grace

Learning from a great Christian's life journey and absorbing their spirit can form us to be more like Christ. Probably the disciple who came to most resemble Jesus is the apostle Paul. The pieces of his story that are dispersed throughout Acts and his letters are summarized in the spiritual biography below to give vision and encouragement for how you can grow spiritually and emotionally in the CHRIST stages of faith.[19]

Confidence in Christ

Saul of Tarsus (later called Paul) was a proud, legalistic, ambitious, and angry Pharisee who took part in the stoning death of Stephen (Acts 7:58; 22:20). He witnessed Stephen talking to Jesus, the one who'd been crucified, and heard Stephen speak words of love and forgiveness over the men who kept pelting him with rocks till he died (Acts 7:54–8:1). Stephen's face had glowed like the face of an angel (Acts 6:15), and it must have burned into Saul's conscience as he replayed Stephen's fiery sermon about Jesus as the Messiah who had risen from the dead.[20] Shortly after this, when Saul was heading to Damascus with a license to kill Christians, the same risen Jesus appeared to him in a bright light. The Lord knocked him off his high horse, blinded him, and spoke words of life to him. Saul put his faith in Jesus and began a radically new life (Acts 9:1–9).

Help in Discipleship

Blind Saul was led by the hand to go to Ananias in Damascus, as Jesus had directed. Ananias taught Saul and prayed for him so that he received the Holy Spirit and his eyes were healed. Ananias introduced Saul to other disciples who encouraged him in his discipleship to Jesus (Acts 9:10–19). Previously, Saul had received extensive religious training in Judaism from his first mentor, Gamaliel (Acts 22:3; Gal. 1:13–14), but now he learned how to interpret the Old Testament in the light of Christ's love for all people and to practice spiritual disciplines like meditation, prayer, worship, fasting, confession of sin, solitude, and Sabbath-keeping as means of grace rather than attempts to earn righteousness.

Later, Barnabas befriended Saul and introduced him to Peter and James in their Jerusalem hideaway that protected them from the religious lynch mob. There he spent fifteen days learning Peter's gospel (Acts 9:26–28; Gal. 1:17–19). For as many as seven years Barnabas mentored Saul.[21]

Responsibilities in Ministry

As an expression of his developing identity as a Christ-follower, Saul traded his Jewish name for his Roman name, Paul. This fit the radical change in his character and his new call from the Lord to bring the gospel to the outsiders.[22] Paul's experience in the stage of Responsibilities in Ministry seems to largely overlap with being in the previous stage of Help in Discipleship. First, as a prominent Pharisee under Gamaliel, he had responsibilities as a teacher of the Law. Then, after his conversion to Christ, he exercised great skill and zeal in preaching the gospel to people in Damascus and Jerusalem (Acts 9:20–22, 28–29).

After Paul encountered The Wall and did some Inner Journey work (described below), it seems he returned to the R Stage when he was immersed in the community of the Antioch church. Under Barnabas' supervision he ministered to people using gifts of service, teaching, and prophecy. This period culminated in Barnabas and Paul being sent out as the first missionary apostles (Acts 11:26; 13:1–3).

The Wall

It seems Paul initially hit The Wall after being badly persecuted by his fellow Jews—first in Damascus and then in Jerusalem. Even the Christians did not trust him and opposed him (Acts 9:23–29). He had been a persecutor of Christians, and now he suffered for his new faith. It was an enormous desolation to him that even though he spent his heart and soul trying to win over his Jewish brothers and sisters to Christ, still they kept rejecting him and even tried to kill him.[23] Apparently, he retreated into three years of solitude in the Arabian desert (Gal. 1:17–18) and then lived hidden away in his hometown of Tarsus for about ten years, probably working as a tentmaker (Acts 9:29–30). He must have wrestled with the Lord: *Why didn't you do what you said? What happened to the promise you made me so many years ago to give me a great ministry?* (Acts 9:15; 26:16–18).

Paul may have re-encountered The Wall during trials later in his journey.[24] For instance, he had been the top Pharisee, but now he was a Johnny-come-lately who was considered to be "the least of the apostles" (1 Cor. 15:8–9) and a boring speaker (2 Cor. 11:6). It was as if Peter and John rolled up in a limousine to admiring crowds and Paul came along later in a jalopy and no one noticed! His ministry was never sufficiently funded, and he had to

54

provide for his own needs by working his fingers to the bone as a tentmaker.[25] On top of all this, he endured attacks from Satan throughout his life.[26]

Inner Journey

In Paul's many "wasted years" during his thirties, when he was either alone in the desert or working as a common tentmaker (Acts 11:25), it seems he developed a deeper bond and discipleship to the risen Christ. We can imagine that, having endured so much rejection and waiting so long for God's promised call to be fulfilled, he had a lot of emotional distress stirring in him and prayed the Psalms as a lifeline. Throughout his many trials he was learning to live the message that the Lord later spoke clearly to him: "My grace is sufficient for you, for my power is made perfect in weakness" (2 Cor. 12:9).

During his many hidden years, and then in the period of deep-spirited community in the Antioch church that followed, Paul developed the joyful devotion to Christ Jesus and the Father that marked his life.[27] It may surprise you that for the first eleven years of Paul's ministry as an apostle he was more of a learner than a leader.[28] He knew that the first priority of his life was not his ministry to others but furthering his own intimacy with God and growing in the character of Christ.

Spirit-Led Ministry

Paul kept immersing himself in God's grace for him as an outsider and sinner, and this enabled him to flourish in sharing the gospel with other outsiders like gentiles, women, and the poor.[29] He became a wounded healer in the way of Jesus (2 Cor. 1:3–7). Previously he had served God by depending on his gifts and the force of his will, but now he learned to live by the Spirit and keep in step with the Spirit (Gal. 5:25). Relying on the Spirit rather than the flesh was a primary teaching of Paul that came out of his own personal experience.[30]

Paul experienced many revelations and visions from God.[31] A typical example of how Paul listened for God's voice and was empowered by the Spirit of grace is when he and his companions were on a mission trip through Phrygia and Galatia and they didn't know where to go next. They trudged through the wilderness toward different villages, but the Spirit of Jesus kept redirecting them. Finally, one night the Spirit gave Paul a dream of a man from Macedonia calling him to cross over the sea to help them (Acts 16:6–10). That's how the gospel got to Europe! Throughout his ministry of preaching, healing, discipling, and establishing churches, Paul did his work in God's power, not his own (1 Cor. 2:4). He operated in the anointing of the Spirit (Acts 19:11–12).

Transforming Union

In all his daily activities and ministry Paul learned to live for the glory of God (1 Cor. 10:31). He prayed without ceasing as much as an imperfect human being can do (1 Thess. 5:17). In all things his single purpose was to embrace Christ (Phil. 3:10, 12). One time he was drawn into union with God in a glorious vision in which he was caught up into the third heaven (2 Cor. 12:2–4).

In his ministry, Paul suffered from continual criticism, the stress of managing all the churches he planted, moonlighting as a tentmaker to support himself, bandits, hunger, sleepless nights out in the cold, and shipwrecks. On top of all this, the religious establishment beat him severely and imprisoned him for bringing God's mercy and justice to outsiders (2 Cor. 11:16–33). Once he was even stoned at Lystra and left for dead, but he popped back up alive (Acts 14:19–20). Apparently, Timothy of Lystra saw Paul love the enemies who stoned him (as Paul had seen Stephen do years earlier). Timothy decided to follow Jesus with Paul and asked to be mentored by him to become a pastor.[32] In all his trials and also in his good times, Paul learned to be content (Phil. 4:12–13). He rejoiced in Christ risen and with him. He forgave his enemies and loved them in Jesus' name. At the end of his life he wrote, "Everyone deserted me. . . . But the Lord stood at my side" (2 Tim. 4:16–17). Even though he had been rejected by his Christian friends and the people he ministered to and was left alone in a cold prison, still he praised God and offered forgiveness and blessings to everyone.[33]

Soul Talk

1. What is one thing you learned in this chapter about God's grace?
2. How does Laura's story relate to you (or a friend)?
3. What helps you move out of the Cycle of Works and into the Cycle of Grace?
4. In the past when you experienced spiritual desolation, what helped you receive grace from God?
5. What is something from Paul's story of grace that is helpful for you?

To support your journey through the CHRIST stages, the upcoming chapters include these special features:

- Story about someone in that stage of faith
- Summary of the stage's key characteristics
- Path Finder questions to see if you are experiencing that stage
- Key developmental dynamics and biblical insights
- Practical suggestions on spiritual disciplines to progress in your journey with Jesus

- Trail Markers highlighting key aspects of that phase
- Guidebook Scriptures to summarize stage themes
- Soul Care Practices with praying Scripture to grow in God's grace
- Soul Talk questions to help you share your journey with friends
- Packing List for the next stage

Packing List for the C Stage

Let's begin the adventure of the CHRIST stages! You've got the big picture of the journey of the soul, so now we want to focus on how to grow in the first stage of Confidence in Christ. Here's what you'll need:

1. Church attendance
2. Hope in God's goodness and love
3. Appreciation that Jesus forgives your sins
4. Playfulness and trust in God (like a child)

3

The C Stage: Confidence in Christ

Following Jesus Christ begins with receiving his forgiveness and new life.

The Lord is my shepherd; I shall not want.

Psalm 23:1 NKJV

L evi was a sixty-year-old Jewish man with a full gray beard, and I (Bill) met him when he was training to serve as a volunteer telephone counselor at the church where I served as a pastor. A while into our conversation he blurted out, "I respect your Christian faith and I like this church, but I can't accept Jesus for myself. My son was a Christian, but he died a year ago." His eyes filled with tears. "Christopher was active in his church and had such a great love for God, like his mother. But after my wife and I divorced and his girlfriend broke up with him, he sank into depression. He swallowed a bottle of pills and that was it . . ."

I invited Levi to share memories of his son. I received the flow of his tears into my heart and God's heart. We celebrated Christopher's life and their relationship. Then Levi asked if his son was in hell because of his suicide, like some people had told him. I contained my anger toward people who would say that and helped Levi articulate his fear at such an awful prospect and *his* anger that anyone would judge his son that way. I shared a few Scriptures about God's mercy and the reasons to believe that Christopher trusted in Jesus' love and forgiveness and was in heaven. Then I suggested that his son might be in the "great cloud of witnesses" praying blessings on Levi right now (Heb. 12:1).

In a later conversation Levi told me about his son's compassion for his friends, people at work, the homeless, and whomever he met. "That's why I want to serve on the hotline in your church," he explained. "It's something Christopher would do. I want to honor his life. Maybe I can take a call from someone who is suicidal and give them hope to keep living." Again, tears streamed down his bearded cheeks.

"Levi, help me understand why if you admire your son's faith in Jesus so much you wouldn't want it for yourself? What has been your experience of God?"

"I'm Jewish like my parents. Christians have told me that my parents aren't in heaven because they didn't believe Jesus was the Messiah."

"I'm sorry. That makes God sound *mean*. Tell me about your parents." He described them and their Jewish faith. I was praying silently about how to respond. I commented, "It sounds like your parents loved you well and they loved God too." Then I asked, "Did they believe in a God of mercy?"

He told me examples of how they depended on Yahweh as their source of forgiveness, love, and wisdom. I explained that it sounded like they had saving faith in the Lord like Abraham, Moses, and others in the Old Testament: they anticipated the coming of the Messiah Jesus by trusting in Yahweh as "the compassionate and gracious God, slow to anger, abounding in love and faithfulness" (Exod. 34:6).

The next time we met, Levi's face was brighter. "I want to pray to receive Jesus as my Savior," he announced. He bounded out of my office that day and onto our hotline the next week. He served Christ faithfully at our church for fifteen years, and God used him as a lifeline for callers who were suicidal.

Characteristics of the C Stage

It's the best news that our Good Shepherd became the Lamb of God, laying down his life to take away our sin (John 1:29; 10:11). "For God so loved the world that he gave his one and only Son, that whoever believes in him shall not perish but have eternal life" (John 3:16). God wants *all people* to be saved (1 Tim. 2:4). "Because Jesus was raised from the dead, we've been given a brand-new life and have everything to live for, including a future in heaven" (1 Pet. 1:3 MSG). We're "born from above" into "a living hope" (John 3:3; 1 Pet. 1:3 YLT). This first stage of Confidence in Christ makes you brand-new like a morning. Later, if you veer off the path or get stuck at The Wall, you'll need to re-enthrall your thoughts with Jesus Christ in the C Stage.

The Bible's prototype for this first CHRIST stage is Abraham, the father of faith for the world's major religions of Judaism, Christianity, and Islam. God declares him righteous and a true friend—not because of anything he does but because he trusts his Lord's promise to bless him in a new land (Gen. 15:6; James 2:23). Abraham has chutzpah[1]—he ventures out into the unknown with audacious belief in his loving Lord. He doesn't even know how to get to the promised land, but he does know Yahweh's presence and voice, so he leads his family and workers there by following the unseen footprints (Ps. 77:19). He perseveres through great difficulties because his faith is not tied to the visible world but to knowing God in spiritual reality (Gen. 11:27–12:5; Heb. 11:1–2, 8–12; in chapter 10 we map out Abraham's life journey). As *bi-habitational beings* we also can learn to live our embodied life in the Kingdom of the Heavens (Matt. 4:17).

Regardless of what physical age we are when we first put faith in our Savior Jesus, at the C Stage we're like children. Child development research shows that faith in God is experiential, relational, and imaginative before it's reasonable.[2] Faith is based on *trust*, which is the first of renowned psychologist Erik Erikson's eight stages of psychosocial development.[3] Trust is established through relationship with a parent (or other caregiver) who is emotionally present, capable, dependable, empathetic, and affirming. In other words, *we need to belong before we can believe.*

Faith Diversity

Your story of faith is precious and unique to you. It's a story that needs to be told, nurtured, and developed. John Newton's story of conversion had a tragic beginning. His mother died when he was a boy, and his father, who was a ship's captain, raised him among vulgar sailors. John became a master of ships and engaged in immorality and the abuses of slave trading. He was trapped in "the slum of sin" (2 Pet. 2:20 MSG) until Jesus Christ set him free and he sang out, "Amazing grace, how sweet the sound that saved a wretch like me!"[4]

C. S. Lewis' story of coming to faith is quite different. As a distinguished professor at Oxford University, he was an agnostic and called his soul his own, but then he felt the "steady, unrelenting approach of Him whom he earnestly desired not to meet." Finally, he says, "I unbuckled my armor and the snow-man started to melt." Ironically, he became "the most reluctant convert in all England." Yet God accepted him with insuppressible grace, and Lewis was "surprised by Joy."[5]

Newton and Lewis received the grace of Christ as adults, but studies show that most people who become Christ-followers do so before age eighteen:[6]

AGE OF ACCEPTING JESUS AS SAVIOR	
Under 13	46%
13 to 17	22%
18 to 29	16%
30 to 49	12%
50 and over	5%

There are many different ways people begin their spiritual journey at the C Stage. Here are some testimonies of young people's emerging faith:

- I (Kristi) was called "Shrimp" as a girl, but when my teacher told me how Jesus loved the "wee little man" Zacchaeus, I ran into Jesus' arms!
- I (Bill) received Jesus as my Lord and Savior as a boy watching a Billy Graham crusade on TV with my parents.
- One of our friends grew up in a "cussin' and drinkin'" home in the Deep South, and he met the Lord through Young Life.
- A Muslim college student from India had never heard about Jesus Christ till he had a dream of a glowing man named Jesus who captivated him with gentle and piercing eyes, so he became a Christ-follower.
- A girl was sexually abused by her father, but she found comfort in her cat snuggling with her and purring, which helped her to trust the God she heard about in Sunday school.
- A high school student responded to an altar call. "My body got all warm and I felt so happy," she reported. "Then all

of a sudden I started praying in a heavenly language and praising the Son of God!"

* A woman prayed to receive Christ as a girl, but in high school she stopped practicing her faith and kept partying and drinking. More than a decade later she started going to Alcoholics Anonymous and recommitted her life to Jesus as her Higher Power.

Path Finder for the C Stage

For each statement below, circle T if it's true of your current experience with God.

YOUR CURRENT EXPERIENCE WITH GOD	TRUE?
1. I'm beginning or renewing my journey as a Christ-follower.	T
2. I'm developing trust that God really loves me.	T
3. I'm learning to admit my need for God's forgiveness, grace, and truth.	T
4. I seek God mostly because I'm hoping for help or to be blessed.	T
5. I'm learning to consistently read the Bible, pray, and go to church.	T
6. I have lots of questions about being a Christian and understanding the Bible.	T
7. I try to follow Jesus' teachings but keep reverting to unhealthy patterns.	T
8. If I try to be still and quiet my mind in prayer, I feel antsy and anxious.	T

If you circled "true" more often for the C Stage than for the other CHRIST stages, this may be your current home stage.

Roadblock: Soul Splits

A rich young man ran up to Jesus, eager to get eternal life. He practiced the Ten Commandments and wanted to serve Yahweh, but Jesus saw that he was holding on tightly to his wealth. His soul was split between two worlds: God and money. The Lord told him that to receive heavenly wealth he'd have to give away his worldly wealth and join his community of disciples. The man's face fell, and he shuffled away with a heavy heart. He missed the wonderful consolation of Jesus looking him right in the eye and loving him (see Mark 10:17–27 MSG).

At the C Stage, our Shepherd is offering us abundant and eternal life, while Satan is vying to steal and destroy that life (John 10:10). We're in a tug-of-war between the kingdoms of light and darkness (Col. 1:13). The devil pulls us into dark lies, pushes us into worldly pleasures, pinches us with guilt trips, and bludgeons us with abuse. In contrast, the Spirit of Grace does not try to force our hand but whispers and woos us with persistent and gentle love. In the battle we're in danger of not seeing our Savior's eyes of love.

Teresa of Jesus explains our soul split as wanting to please His Majesty and perform good works but getting "absorbed in worldly affairs, engulfed in worldly pleasures, and puffed up with worldly honors and ambitions."[7] We keep "falling into sins and rising from them again," going back and forth between the sweet voice of the Savior and the "haggling" temptations of the world.[8] James calls this being "two-souled" (1:8; 4:8 YLT). He says we're doubting God's goodness, which makes us like a rudderless sailboat at sea that's driven and tossed back and forth by the shifting winds of sinful desires (1:6).

Peter also was torn between two worlds. When he asserted with bravado that he'd never deny Jesus, the Savior urged him, "Watch and pray so that you will not fall into temptation. The spirit is willing, but the flesh is weak" (Mark 14:38). Peter's *heart* (spirit) was determined to be faithful to Jesus, but his *flesh* (natural human ability) was habituated in pride and anger. He had a soul split. Jesus' remedy (spiritual discipline) was for Peter to watch and pray with him in the garden. In this way Peter could join Jesus' intimacy with Abba and submission to God, which would enable him to deny his worldly ambition (14:36). But Peter kept falling asleep, so his torn soul was not repaired and he could not carry out the good desire of his heart (vv. 37, 40, 41).

Later Peter *did* learn to watch and pray and be faithful to his Master, so his split soul was made whole (Acts 1:14–15; 2:1). What helped him to be loyal to his Lord? He saw Jesus look into his soul with penetrating love (Luke 22:61; John 21:15–17).

Jesus looks at you with those same eyes of love! Even now you can make eye contact with Jesus . . .

Thank you, Lord, that your mercies are fresh and new every morning![9]

Grace: Sticky Love

Consider this story of a small child whose soul is vulnerable to splitting. Two-year-old Tommy is playing in a sandbox at a park while his mom sits on a bench about ten feet away. As he plays independently, now and again he looks back to see if his mother is still watching him: *Is this okay? Are you here for me?* If she were to frown or look worried then he'd feel insecure and anxious. But she smiles as if to say, *Yes, honey, I'm right here—you're safe. And I love the castle you're making!* (It's really a lumpy hill, but she sees a castle.) So he continues playing. Even without touching or using any words they're staying connected emotionally.

Suddenly, a train roars and rumbles down the tracks adjacent to the park! The loud horn and shaking ground crash into Tommy's soul and frighten him. Instantly, he rushes over to his mom, and she scoops him up into her lap and holds him close. She helps him cover his ears to quiet down the loud noise. Then, when the train is gone, he looks up at his mom, and she smiles at him and verbalizes his feelings. "That sure was loud and scary, wasn't it, Tommy?" Then she kisses him softly on the cheek as they continue to snuggle. After a minute or so he wiggles down and goes back to exploring and playing in his sandbox world nearby. He's refueled emotionally through his mother's empathy, so his momentary soul split is repaired, and he is strengthened to return to joy and confidence.[10]

Tommy's mother is caring for him with God's *hessed*, which is Hebrew for "sticky love." Psalm 63 is one of 248 times the Old Testament ministers sticky love to foster our trust in God. David sings, "Yahweh, your stick-to-it love is better than living. . . . So my soul [embodied life] clings to you" (vv. 3, 8).[11] The psychological term for sticky love is *secure attachment*. Over time, the mirror neurons in Tommy's brain have been helping him to mimic and internalize his mother's love and to stay attached to her even in stress and pain.[12] This is not only a matter of comfort; infants who are provided basic sustenance but are not held, caressed, mirrored, or spoken to in loving tones can actually die.[13] Conversely, research shows that loving touch and warm presence lead to increases in oxytocin and endorphins that enhance bonding, well-being, and health.[14] Better yet, empathy inspires us to trust the Lord Jesus as our refuge.

When we sin or get hurt, our gut-level faith in our Savior is seen in how we respond. If we deny our sin or emotions, go into our head, get busy, or turn to addictive behaviors, then we're relationally detaching from the Spirit of truth and grace. Instead, if we share personally with God and an empathetic friend, then we can release the toxicity of sin and distress (like fear, anxiety, depression, shame, anger, and bitterness) and receive Christ's love, joy, peace, and courage. Empathy is vastly underappreciated—it's a palpable way that the Holy Spirit ministers to us the sticky love of Christ that restores our soul splits.

Looking into Jesus' Face to Trust God

In my (Bill's) dissertation for a PhD in psychology, I studied the connection between God-images and self-images, because A. W. Tozer wrote that "what comes into our minds when we think about God is the most important thing about us."[15] In fact, research shows that our God-image is so powerful that it fosters changes in our brain circuits.[16] Often we think our image of God is limited to our concepts and beliefs, but actually it's less about our theology and more about our *knee*-ology. How we actually feel and experience God when we pray is largely based on our early childhood relationships. Emotional wounds, love deficits, and sin can adversely affect how we relate to and experience God.

What do you see when you look into God's face? Many see a frown or a blank stare. It's as if God is a cop in the sky or a stone-faced statue. Others see God like a magic genie who will grant their prayer requests, but only if they say the right words.

Jesus Christ shows us the true face of God, but in a picture book that features ninety-five famous paintings of Jesus' face from the fourteenth to the twentieth centuries, only one shows him smiling.[17] *Only one.* Even as our Savior preaches the Good News and heals the sick, he is portrayed as a somber religious man. It's true that Jesus was "a man of sorrows, and acquainted with grief" (Isa. 53:3 KJV), but that was not his usual demeanor. A veil of solemn religiosity has obscured our view of the friendly and resplendent Son of God who prays for us to be *full of his joy* (Luke 10:21; John 15:11; 17:13). In fact, Jesus was so happy to be with people and bless them that in the Gospels we keep seeing people *running* to him![18]

Clearly, Jesus shows us that *God is not mean!* When we see God angry in the Bible, it's not like most human anger. It's an expression of love for the abused—and the abuser. When God seems distant, it's to draw us closer. When God's love seems conditional or only for the privileged, we're not appreciating *Jesus on the cross with his arms open to forgive every person* (2 Cor. 5:15). That's the ultimate sticky love!

How can we renew our heartfelt image of God as being exactly like Jesus? How can we develop confident, enduring faith in a God who is totally beautiful, good, just, forgiving, and compassionate? The standard approach of didactic teaching is not enough—we also need sticky love relationships. Psychology of religion author James Fowler warns that if parents or teachers insist that children (and other spiritual beginners) have orthodox beliefs, it's premature and damaging. The best way for children and adults to cultivate heart trust in God is by accessing their emotional brain along with their rational brain. We do this by relating with loving guides, imagining ourselves in Bible stories (especially with Jesus in the Gospels), and interacting personally with tangible Christian symbols like the cross, water baptism, candles, and the bread and cup.[19]

In the deepest part of our personality, we're all like children, with insecurities and hopes. That's why no matter what age we are, the Lord Jesus calls us to come to him in God's kingdom in the same way Tommy trusted his mother's empathy and strength (Matt. 18:2–4). Trusting in God's kindness to you is what activates and guides you to make positive changes in your life (Rom. 2:4). The Lord is our deliverer, healer, and provider before being our lawgiver.[20] We're correcting our heart image of God as totally loving by "fixing our eyes on Jesus, the pioneer and perfecter of faith" (Heb. 12:2).

Here are some practical steps for cultivating C-Stage trust in Christ's unfailing love:

1. Imagine yourself in a favorite story about Jesus (it may help to use a children's Bible).
2. Look at a picture of yourself as a child and pray to the Father of Jesus about how you felt.
3. Sing a praise song to God like an enthusiastic child using hand motions or dancing a little.
4. Take turns sharing childhood memories with a friend, being careful to listen with empathy.
5. Smile to God as a prayer of love (see the soul care practice below).

·················· Trail Markers for the C Stage ··················

AGE	3 to adult
FAITH	Hope and trust
COGNITIVE DEVELOPMENT	Experiential and imaginative
ROADBLOCK & TEMPTATIONS	Soul splits (e.g., seeking to love God but falling in sin) Black-and-white categorizing (dualism) Seeking worldly pleasures and addictions Denying sin, struggle, and stress Projecting negative experiences onto God Disbelieving the reality of God (agnosticism)
IMAGES OF GOD	Jesus as Savior and God as loving Father
GRACE	Sticky love (and forgiveness)
LESSONS	Trusting in the Father's love through Jesus Christ Participating in church Admitting brokenness and need for grace and truth Asking God for blessings Seeking to obey Bible teachings
SPIRITUAL DISCIPLINES	Attending church Noticing God in nature Learning from spiritual leaders Reading Bible stories (especially the Gospels) Praying about personal needs Christian devotionals, podcasts, books, etc. Gratitude for God's blessings Singing praise songs to God Submission to the sovereign Lord Confession of sin and dysfunction Baptism and communion
CHURCH MINISTRIES	Administration (many functions) Childcare Hospitality (e.g., ushering) Serving on worship team Sharing your testimony Serving communion

· · · · · · · · · · · · · **Guidebook Scriptures for the C Stage** · · · · · · · · · · · · ·

- **You're chosen by Father God:** "You are not forgotten, for you have been chosen and destined by Father God. . . . May God's delightful grace and peace cascade over you many times over! Celebrate with praises the God and Father of our Lord Jesus Christ. . . . For his fountain of mercy has given us a new life . . . through the resurrection of Jesus Christ from the dead" (1 Pet. 1:2–3 TPT).

- **Put hope in God's good plans:** "'I know the plans I have for you,' declares the LORD, 'plans to prosper you and not to harm you, plans to give you hope and a future'" (Jer. 29:11).

- **Trust God's love:** "GOD is sheer mercy and grace; not easily angered, he's rich in love" (Ps. 103:8 MSG).

- **Confess brokenness to be healed:** "Confess your sins to each other and pray for each other so that you may be healed" (James 5:16).

- **Seek God's blessings:** "Without faith it is impossible to please God, because anyone who comes to him must believe that he exists and that he rewards those who earnestly seek him" (Heb. 11:6).

- **Be nourished in God's Word:** "Like newborn babies, crave pure spiritual milk, so that by it you may grow up in your salvation" (1 Pet. 2:2).

- **Keep learning:** "Though the righteous fall seven times, they rise again" (Prov. 24:16).

Soul Care Practice

Delighting in the Lord

For me (Kristi) life at home felt like Grand Central Station when we had three teenagers. So Bill and I periodically blessed each other with extended hours of TLC time ("To Love Christ") for rest, reflection, and solitary prayer. One day it was my turn, and I headed to the beach. I'd like to invite you into my experience:

> My busy home life faded away as I sat on the sand with my Bible and journal open, soaking up the sunshine, listening to the waves roll in. I came across a verse in the Psalms I'd never noticed before: "Give [God] your warmest smile" (Ps. 34:5 MSG). *I've never done that,* I realized. I'd never intentionally smiled to Jesus. So that's what I did—all day! I read my Bible and journaled my prayers. I especially cried out to God on behalf of one of our teens who was challenging us. I let God's ocean permeate my soul. I napped. In all this I stayed happy by purposefully *smiling* my love to God like a girl to her daddy. (We adults need to become more childlike, because we smile just twenty times a day, but children smile *four hundred* times a day![21])

Even in difficult or unjust circumstances we have a source of joy. Some time ago a friend gave us a little book titled *The Happy Texts*, which features 122 of the more than 800 "rejoicing passages" in the Bible. Reading those happy texts makes our hearts happy in God—really happy! We can pray verses like "Celebrate God all day, every day. I mean *revel* in him!" (Phil. 4:4 MSG). We get carried by wave after wave of the Lord and his angels blessing us with pleasure, laughter, cheer, rejoicing, gladness, delight, and merrymaking. It's not that we are creating a consolation experience—that is the work of the Spirit of Jesus. Rather, it's a discipline for opening ourselves to be in a posture to receive an outpouring of God's grace.

Smiling a Prayer

Inspired by my smiling prayer, Bill composed a breath prayer from the Bible: "Jesus delights in me . . . I delight in you, my Lord . . ." (Pss. 18:19; 34:5; 37:4).[22] Even when you're emotional or needy or when you've sinned, *Jesus delights to know you and care for you.* Try going through this prayer rhythm:

- Sit, stand, or walk in a quiet place . . .
- Imagine Jesus smiling, and smile back . . .
- Breathe in deeply and slowly, over and over . . .
- Breathe in: "Jesus delights in me . . ."
- Breathe out: "I delight in you, my Lord . . ."
- Gently repeat this rhythm for a few minutes . . .

What a blessing it is when Jesus' smile plays on your face and prays in your soul! Over the years we've shared the "Jesus delights in me" prayer with thousands of people, and many are taken aback: *Jesus is happy to see me! He doesn't just love me because he has to—he actually delights in me and sings a love song over me!*[23] Some people begin to cry with joy. Many put a picture of a smiling Jesus on their bathroom mirror or phone.[24] Perhaps taking a few breaths and smiling a Bible-based prayer to Jesus Christ sounds too simple to have such a big impact, but with practice you'll see it will truly bless you and the people around you with God's delightful love.[25]

Soul Talk

1. Why is it important to begin our faith journey trusting in God as merciful and gracious?
2. What do you think about the idea that we are torn between the kingdoms of Christ and Satan?
3. What helps you appreciate that God's sticky love is better than anything else in life (Ps. 63:3)?
4. Which is your favorite Guidebook Scripture for the C Stage? How could this strengthen your faith?
5. What was your experience with smiling and breathing the prayer "Jesus delights in me"?

Packing List for the H Stage

God has new blessings for you in the next stage of Help in Discipleship. To develop in this stage you'll need:

1. Good Bible teaching
2. Respect for Jesus as your Teacher
3. Gratitude for God's blessings
4. Church community

The H Stage:
Help in Discipleship

We grow by being in community with Christ-followers and practicing spiritual disciplines.

> He makes me to lie down in green pastures;
> He leads me beside the still waters.
> He restores my soul.
>
> Psalm 23:2–3 NKJV

Amanda prayed to receive Jesus Christ as her Savior in junior high, but she didn't learn how to grow in her relationship with him. She explained, "I read the Bible but I couldn't understand it. I wanted to live like a Christian, but I also wanted to have the attention of the popular girls, so I became like them." She continued to be distracted through her school years and after getting married and having children, but then her husband lost his job. "We didn't know how to keep putting food on the table for our family," she recalled. "A neighbor across the street supported me and invited me to her church. Our whole family found a place of belonging and acceptance there. The pastor told us, 'When one part of the body suffers, the whole body suffers.' I couldn't believe it when checks started showing up in the mail!"

Amanda and her husband joined a Bible study group for couples at church, which encouraged their faith. "I read about God's promises to care for us," she recalled. "It was like the Bible was speaking right to me—I couldn't get enough! I read voraciously and took hold of the blessings that go with being Jesus' disciple."

Life really improved for Amanda and her family. Her husband made a connection at church that helped him to get a great job. Their church provided opportunities for them to make new friends and learn biblical teaching on topics like managing money, marriage, parenting, and spiritual disciplines. Her story illustrates the findings of studies showing that church-based relationships have a positive impact on our health and well-being, even more than other relationships.[1]

Characteristics of the H Stage

The Psalm 23 journey illustrates that the sweet sufficiency of Good Shepherd coaxes us first to trust him in the C Stage and then to follow him into the H Stage. He's leading us onward to graze in his green pastures of grace and drink from his still waters of love that restore our soul (vv. 2–3). The Shepherd's consolations for us cultivate the sticky-love bond that is the basis for us to learn and be led in the stage of Help in Discipleship. To be clear, we don't mean to suggest that discipleship is a stage, because actually it's our *whole life*. Instead, the H Stage focuses on being cared for and guided by an ambassador for Christ who ministers God's friendship and wisdom (2 Cor. 5:20). According to Teresa of Jesus, it's essential at this stage of our journey that we are in "close touch" with disciples of Jesus who are more spiritually mature than we are.[2]

For many Christians, their early growth in grace is an exciting season of learning the Bible with other Christ-followers. Often a local church is the catalyst and context for the H Stage, but it may be a parachurch ministry, mission organization, 12-step group, or other spiritual community. We're affiliating with people who share our beliefs and values, and this gives us belonging, security, and identity. Like Ruth in the Bible, we say to our new friends and teachers, "I will go where you go and stay where you stay. Your people will be my people and your God will be my God" (see Ruth 1:16).

In the H Stage we ask lots of basic questions: *Who is Jesus? How can I be sure that I'm saved? Can I trust the Bible? Do I need to join a church? What does this Scripture mean? How do I pray?* We have so much to learn! We look to pastors and other teachers for answers and help in learning to obey the Bible. We may participate in small groups, Bible studies, choir, youth camps, classes on Christian doctrine or spirituality, retreats, mission trips, or social justice causes. We learn to use disciplines for spiritual growth like daily Bible reading, prayer, worship, tithing, creeds, memorizing verses and promises in the Bible, quiet times, spiritual warfare, serving, and sharing our faith.

Our mindset in the H Stage and the First Half of our journey is to think in very concrete terms and categorize life in dualistic ideas of black and white, good or bad, and us versus them.[3] We expect life to be linear, predictable, reciprocal, fair. We want secure orientation and equilibrium and to believe that our righteousness is rewarded: *If I sow good seed then I'll reap a good harvest* (Deut. 28:1–2; Gal. 6:7). It's the Proverbs life in which all who listen and obey the voice of wisdom "will live in safety and be at ease, without fear of harm" (1:33).[4] This mentality is *generally* true, and it helps those who are younger in age or faith to progress in their Christian growth. However, it also makes us prone to legalism and judgmentalism. The law is a good guardian, but if we try to measure up to it in our own power, then it becomes a religious system of reproach.[5]

Some Christians get stuck in the H Stage in a rule-focused, dualistic orientation that restricts their enjoyment of God's grace and their capacity to give grace to other people (we'll discuss this further in chapter 6). But we want to be like Mary Magdalene, who in the H Stage kept growing closer to her beloved Teacher and gave him the affectionate nickname "Rabboni" (John 20:16). She progressed in her faith and became a leader in the early church.[6]

Here are some testimonies of people who are growing in the H Stage:

- "The Bible verses I memorized as a child in AWANA help me as a student."
- "In high school a friend invited me into an Alpha group at her church, and we had conversations about faith and culture that drew me to follow Jesus."
- "I'm growing through my pastor's sermons and insightful teachings about life, morality, and family."
- "The leader of my community Bible study group disciples me. I have lots of questions, and she directs me to God's wisdom."
- "I started really growing in my faith when I got involved in our church's Serve ministry and met with the leaders for prayer before going out to minister."
- "I was Hindu when I attended an ESL class at a church, and I met some friendly Christians and heard Bible stories that made me trust Jesus as the Son of God."
- "Learning about spiritual disciplines is exciting! It's really helping me to draw closer to Christ."

Path Finder for the H Stage

For each statement below, circle T if it's true of your current experience with God.

YOUR CURRENT EXPERIENCE WITH GOD	TRUE?
1. I'm discovering the right things to believe from the Bible.	T
2. Participating in church activities is important for my spiritual growth.	T
3. I'm growing by following the teachings of my spiritual leader(s).	T
4. I'm learning spiritual disciplines that help me to follow Christ.	T
5. If everyone had my beliefs, they'd be assured of their salvation.	T
6. My group of friends is helping me grow as a disciple of Jesus.	T
7. I seek to obey God's wisdom because it blesses me.	T
8. It's hard for me to be quiet and still in prayer for long.	T

If you circled "true" more often for the H Stage than the other CHRIST stages, this may be your current home stage.

Roadblock: Misinterpreting Scripture

Dallas Willard teaches, "We live at the mercy of our ideas."[7] But we need to understand that *most of our ideas are unconscious and laden with emotion.* Emotions often get minimized in discipleship, but they're just as important as thinking. Renewing our mind in God's tender mercy includes dealing with our thoughts and feelings (Rom. 12:1–2).[8] Neuroscience research validates that "we feel before we think, and if we don't feel we can't actually think."[9] When we integrate feeling and thinking, our Christian doctrines inspire us to dance with Jesus as we serve in his Kingdom of Love!

Neglecting to think about our spiritual feelings and feel about our spiritual thoughts causes some common biblical blunders that undermine God's grace. The H Stage is a prime time to scrub these untrue and unhealthy feeling-thought patterns.

1. Be perfect

Jesus' words to "be perfect, therefore, as your heavenly Father is perfect" (Matt. 5:48) are easily misinterpreted by eager disciples at the H Stage. The greatest Rabbi is not endorsing religious perfectionism. Rather, he warns against this, saying we'll end up straining gnats and swallowing a camel (Matt. 23:24).

Human willpower for doing disciplines and moral muscle for keeping rules have the appearance of wisdom, but they're not enough to sustain loving attitudes and behaviors (Col. 2:23). It's a self-help project of relying too much on our own abilities and energies and not enough on the Spirit of Jesus. This can lead to being prideful, dogmatic, legalistic, pharisaical, and judgmental. This is why God declares that our self-made righteous actions are nothing but "filthy rags" and urges us to rest in our Father's loving hands to be shaped, like a potter sculpting soft clay (Isa. 64:6, 8).

2. Do not feel anxious

Christopher was taught in his family and church that it was a *sin* to be anxious. He explained, "I repressed my negative emotions by reciting Bible verses and trying to stay positive all the time. As an adult I bought a Christian book on anxiety that reinforced this thinking. My wife, kids, and friends kept telling me they felt controlled and criticized, but I didn't listen. I was always trying to get them to look and act right, like me. I was living in my head—*my faith never touched my feelings.*"

In our Soul Shepherding Institute, Christopher learned about empathy and *he experienced it.* He was surprised to discover that when Paul says, "Do not be anxious" in Philippians 4, he is not saying do not *feel* anxious. He's saying in effect, "*Whenever* you feel stressed or worried, talk to God about how you feel, sharing your emotions openly. Don't pretend to be strong—be vulnerable. Ask for the grace you need and be sure to receive it by being thankful. Then God's sweet and powerful peace will nourish and protect you in the way of Christ" (Phil. 4:6–7, authors' paraphrase).

3. Just have faith

Some excited followers of Christ Jesus latch onto his promises to answer prayer, believing if they just "have faith" or "pray in Jesus' name" then they'll get whatever they ask for (Matt. 21:22). Unconsciously, they're projecting their desires and linear mindset into the Bible, treating it like a contract where if they do something good then God has to bless them.

Praying in Jesus' name or claiming a Bible promise is not like putting money in a vending machine or saying a magic incantation. In the Bible a person's name reflects their character, so to pray in Jesus' name means to pray in a way that is consistent with his submission to God and compassion for people. If our prayers are not answered, the Teacher encourages us to persevere in praying to our loving Father, trusting that good things will eventually come to us (Luke 11:5–13).

4. Hate yourself

When she was in the H Stage, Shannon believed the Bible taught her to hate herself. When she was growing up, her parents were drug addicts and threw wild parties where some of their groupies violated her sexually. As a young adult Shannon's shame and sexualized identity led her to become a porn star in order to get enough money to move away from her parents. Then a Christian woman befriended her and invited her to church where she met friendly people who didn't judge her, accepted her story, and treated her with dignity. She found belonging in her church and soaked up the Bible, but she despised her past, her body, and her emotional needs. She misused Jesus' words about hating our life to *shame herself*. But the Master Teacher's point is that our devotion to God needs to be so singular and intense that in comparison it's *as if* we hate our self (John 12:25–26).

Similarly, to deny yourself does not mean to *negate* yourself but to replace inferior worldly desires with heavenly desires that will bless you and others (Luke 9:23–25).[10] For Shannon, releasing feelings and thoughts of shame helped her to appreciate and absorb the healing grace that God and her church friends were giving her.

Willpower Is Not Enough

Some years ago I (Bill) did a triathlon with a one-mile swim, 25-mile bike ride, and 10K run. I was very slow on the swim, so when I got to the bike ride I was at the back of the pack. I pounded on the pedals and soared down the highway at twenty miles an hour, passing lots of bikers. That was fun! But then my chain fell off. I had to pull over to the side of the road, turn my bike upside down, get my fingers all greasy, and mess with the chain to get it back onto the chain ring. Meanwhile, streams of bikers were passing by me. I got back on my bike and pounded on the pedals and passed people again. But then my chain fell off again! I had to do the same routine: turn my bike upside down, get greasy, and put the chain back on. Of course, bikers were flying by me again. As before, I got back on my bike and pounded on the pedals. Now I was passing the same bikers *for the third time*. One guy looked over at me, just inches from my face, and exclaimed, "Man, you're strong . . . but *stupid!*"

In the H Stage we're prone to be strong but stupid, having zeal without knowledge (Prov. 19:2). I was unwise not to prepare my bike, so even though I ran a good race to finish the triathlon, my finishing time was much slower than it could've been.

Another case in point is the story about a man's uncle who waited till he retired from his career to get serious about growing in his faith. In his first year of retirement he read the Bible from beginning to end. After this success he set out to read the entire Bible in a single month, which takes two-and-a-half hours per day. He did it! He determined to keep this pace to read through the Bible cover-to-cover every month for the rest of his life. In twelve years he read the whole Bible 144 times! Then he died.

Not many people have done so much Bible reading, and yet the man who observed his uncle's Bible-reading marathon reported, "Here's the irony: my uncle died the meanest, bitterest son of a gun you'd ever wish to meet!"[11] The cranky uncle's strong will for Bible reading didn't make him like Jesus. He was strong but stupid because he kept getting through the Bible, but *he didn't let the Bible get through him.* He didn't open his heart to let the Word of God and the Holy Spirit inspire him to confess his sins, ask forgiveness, and learn how to share God's love with people. He got stuck in the Cycle of Works and missed the Cycle of Grace and the Christlike character it fuels.

Grace: God's Word in Community

The relationships and Bible teachings of my church have been central to my (Kristi's) growth in the stage of Help in Discipleship. When I was a child, my family went to church services three days a week. My church was like a second family for me. I had friends, older children, and teachers who were role models and encouragers to me. At church I belonged—I felt safe, loved, wanted, cared for, and affirmed—and this enabled me to learn so much about being a Christ-follower. I especially enjoyed the children's club where I earned prizes for memorizing Bible verses and the choir where we sang songs from Scripture. I went to church camps where we had contests to see who could look up Bible verses the fastest, recite the most memory verses, and answer spiritual questions. We acted out Bible stories and pledged allegiance to the Christian flag. I was proud to invite my friends from school and the neighborhood to come to church with me.

My growth in grace continued in the high school group at church, as well as at Christian conferences and seminars. Prayer and reading the Bible helped me to feel confident of God's love for me. In school I felt lots of peer pressure to compromise my values and do what the popular kids were doing, but thankfully my family and church relationships helped me stay faithful to Christ. This protected me from much pain and harm, but I did struggle with feeling isolated and depressed. Throughout my years as a student, new wife, and mother of young children, I continued to find consolation in my church, faith, and devotional practices.

I (Bill) also have found support in my church for my growth as a Christ-follower. One prominent example was in my early thirties when I revisited the spiritual training aspects of the H Stage after spending more than a decade in the R and I Stages. I joined a year-long discipleship group led by Ray Ortlund Sr., the church's former senior pastor. "Let's rub up our lives together in Christ's presence," was Ray's invitation to us. "Jesus withdrew to be with his disciples, and that's what we're going to do." He called this *life-on-life discipleship*.

As a group we opened God's Word and our daily planners, shared our personal concerns, and prayed for one another. We gathered for meetings, meals, retreats, and ministry events. I also met with Ray privately for spiritual direction once a month for a number of years. Ray was a megachurch pastor, bestselling author, radio personality, and missionary who had spoken to 200,000 people at one time. But in our group he was just one of the guys opening his heart and his Bible. He was so real and free and fun that one time over lunch he prayed for me, "Lord, bless Bill's praying life, his laughing life, and his sex life with his wife!"

Being mentored is the *H* in Help in Discipleship. "Every Christian needs some older Christian they're learning from and some younger Christian they're teaching," Ray exhorted us.[12] We see this spiritual relay race in Paul's life: Barnabas discipled Paul, Paul discipled Timothy, and Timothy discipled others (2 Tim. 2:2). In Ray's discipleship group I learned how to live my life as Jesus would if he were me. I also learned Jesus' pattern of replication: he ministered and they watched, they ministered with him and he watched, and he sent them out two-by-two on mission and they reported back. So that's what we did. We watched Ray lead our group and his other ministries. He watched and supported each of us in our ministries, including taking turns leading our group. Then he sent us out to lead our own discipleship groups and cheered us on from the sidelines.

Don't Try—Train

Adam was in his twenties and wanted to be like Jesus, but pornography kept pulling him out of the H Stage and back into the split soul of the C Stage. No matter how hard he tried to be pure, he kept falling. Church, life group, Bible study, meeting with an accountability partner—nothing was working. His discipleship program was not helping him get free of the porn trap because he was white-knuckling the steering wheel of his life. His lust problem was really a love deficit. He was not experiencing a sticky love relationship with his Savior that satisfied his soul. He needed to apply the motto "Don't try—train" (see 1 Tim. 4:7), which is the opposite of being strong but stupid. It means asking Jesus to coach you in using some key disciplines as means of grace.[13]

The first goal of Adam's training was to help him set his heart on the radiant Son of God. He needed to become like the man who found treasure hidden in a field and was so ecstatic that he sold everything to buy the field (Matt. 13:44). That's how wonderful it is to join your daily life to Jesus in the Kingdom of the Heavens.

Secondly, Adam needed to seek empathy for his broken emotional self. It's easy to forget that *trusting Jesus is connected to trusting his friends.* For Adam's recovery he practiced being vulnerable and receiving empathetic listening and grace from the Lord through me and his 12-step group.

Additionally, Adam's previous habit of lusting needed to be replaced with a new habit of finding sweet sufficiency in Christ (Col. 3:5, 11). To establish a new conscious override mechanism, I taught him to pray, "Your love, O Lord, is better than lust" (an application of Ps. 63:3). At the same time, he periodically fasted from food while feasting (meditating) on Scripture. Once he learned he could go without food for a meal or more and still be physically and emotionally well cared for by God, then he could apply that to break free of lust. That's using indirection with spiritual disciplines: you're doing something *you can do* (fast from food) in order to learn to do something *you can't yet do* (resist lust).

Whenever Satan lured him, Adam would begin to pray God's Word to help him praise the Lord Jesus and pray blessings on the person he was tempted to lust after (Rom. 12:21). Love for God and others had replaced lust at the center of his heart. (Chapter 7 on the Inner Journey features extended discussion on cultivating a heart for God.)

As with Adam, in whatever life problems you have, the basic soul-shepherding program is to follow the Triangle of Soul Transformation that enables us to live and work in Jesus' easy yoke:

1. Fix your thoughts and affections on the sufficiency of Christ.

2. Seek empathy for your particular struggle from the Lord and a friend.

3. Use disciplines to develop new habits of loving God and people.[14]

················· **Trail Markers for the H Stage** ·················

AGE	7 to adult
FAITH	Belonging and learning
COGNITIVE DEVELOPMENT	Concrete and linear
ROADBLOCK & TEMPTATIONS	Misinterpreting Scripture Spiritual zeal without knowledge Legalism; spiritual perfectionism Expecting that if you do good God should bless you Forming cliques; us versus them Judging yourself as less than or superior to others
IMAGES OF GOD	Jesus as Teacher and Coach
GRACE	God's Word in community
LESSONS	Learning foundational Bible teachings Belonging in a church or other Christian community Asking faith questions of spiritual teachers Learning spiritual disciplines Developing habits for trusting Jesus in daily life
SPIRITUAL DISCIPLINES	Daily devotions (e.g., the One Year Bible) Being discipled to Jesus by a pastor or teacher Getting involved in church (or spiritual community) Praying the Lord's Prayer Memorizing Bible verses Participating in a small group Reading the New Testament Spiritual warfare (resisting Satan's lies and distractions) Serving others and seeking social justice
CHURCH MINISTRIES	Shepherding students Discipling new believers (with curriculum) Prayer ministry

··········· Guidebook Scriptures for the H Stage ·············

- **Jesus is the Discipler:** "Jesus said, 'If you hold to my teaching, you are really my disciples. Then you will know the truth, and the truth will set you free'" (John 8:31–32).

- **The Bible is our curriculum:** "Every Scripture has been written by the Holy Spirit, the breath of God. It will empower you by its instruction and correction, giving you the strength to take the right direction and lead you deeper into the path of godliness" (2 Tim. 3:16 TPT).

- **Your local church is a blessing:** "Some people have gotten out of the habit of meeting for worship, but we must not do that. We should keep on encouraging each other" (Heb. 10:25 CEV).

- **Find a mentor and group for growth:** "Ten [people] from different nations . . . will clutch at the sleeve of one Jew. And they will say, 'Please let us walk with you, for we have heard that God is with you'" (Zech. 8:23 NLT).

- **Ask spiritual questions:** God says, "Call to me and I will answer you. I'll tell you marvelous and wondrous things that you could never figure out on your own" (Jer. 33:3 MSG).

- **Obey God's Word and be blessed:** "Keep my commands in your heart, for they will prolong your life many years and bring you peace and prosperity" (Prov. 3:1–2).

- **Practice disciplines:** "Exercise daily in God—no spiritual flabbiness, please!" (1 Tim. 4:7 MSG).

- **Do what is right, avoid what is wrong:** "Turn your back on evil, work for the good and don't quit. GOD loves this kind of thing, never turns away from his friends" (Ps. 37:27–28 MSG).

Soul Care Practice

Jesus' Pocket Lighter

Jesus' disciples watched him pray. They heard him call God "Papa" (Mark 14:36 MSG). They saw that his praying life gave him unmatched compassion and wisdom, the power to heal people and calm storms, and the ability to love his enemies with ease. So they asked him, "Lord, teach us to pray" (Luke 11:1). This was not a polite petition but an urgent cry of the heart: *Lord, teach us to pray!* They longed for the life they saw in him.

Then the Messiah and Master shared *his personal prayer.* He wasn't just giving us his words—he gave us his way. He's teaching us *how* to pray by giving us the key that opens our Psalms prayer book, for as Dietrich Bonhoeffer once said, "The Lord's Prayer is the Psalms in miniature."[15] Jesus spent his whole life praying the treasury of David, and then he distilled the essence of all 150 of its prayers into five categories of petitions for living as his disciple in the Kingdom of God.

To ask God for what we and others need is not necessarily immature as some suppose. In Jesus' great sermons on prayer he taught that prayer is essentially making sincere requests of our Father with persistence, and he emphasized that this requires giving and receiving forgiveness for sins (Matt. 6:5–7:12; Luke 11:1–13, 18:1–8).

How Luther Prayed

One day Martin Luther's barber asked him how he prayed. Luther told him he used the Lord's Prayer, and he spelled out what this looked like in a *forty-page handwritten letter*! It was later published and became an all-time classic.

> *Dear Master Peter,*
>
> *I give you the best I have. I tell you how I pray myself. May our Lord God grant you and everyone to do it better.*
>
> *A good clever barber must have his thoughts, mind and eyes concentrated upon the razor and the beard and not forget where he is in his stroke and shave. If he keeps talking or looking around or thinking of something else, he is likely to cut a man's mouth or nose—or even his throat! . . . How much more must prayer possess the heart exclusively and completely if it is to be a good prayer!*[16]

Luther was famous by this time, but he put himself on Peter's level by admitting, "When I feel that I have become cool and joyless in prayer because of other tasks or thoughts (for the flesh and the devil always impede and obstruct prayer), I take my little psalter, hurry to my room, or, if it be the day and hour for it, to the church where a congregation is assembled."[17]

He tells his barber that he listens to the Spirit as he prays. "One word of his sermon is far better than a thousand of our prayers. Many times I have learned more from one prayer than I might have learned from much reading and speculation."[18] This is not only intellectual learning—it's also *emotional and relational bonding*. He says, "I suckle at the Lord's Prayer like a child."[19] Similarly, he urges us, "I want your heart to be stirred" by using Jesus' prayer "as a pocket lighter to kindle a flame in the heart."[20] Like a dog chewing a bone, we're praying Scripture slowly, meditatively, reflectively. We're personalizing the phrases as heartfelt intercessions for ourselves and others. We might even memorize Jesus' prayer and pray through it each day.

Praying Jesus' Pocket Lighter

I paraphrased the Lord's Prayer and often use this fresh wording to luxuriate myself in it.[21] May these renewed prayer-words be a pocket lighter to warm your heart for God:

> Our Father in the heavens, always near and ready to help,
> May your name be precious to us and bring us delight always.
> May your Kingdom of the Heavens come to rule over us
> So your good, pleasing, and perfect will is accomplished in us.
> Please provide for us the food and care that we need today.
> Please forgive our sins as we forgive those who have sinned
> against us.
> Please hold us by the hand so we don't fall down in trials
> And are kept safe from all evil.
> In everything help us to live *in* your kingdom, *by* your
> power, and *for* your glory.
> Amen. (Matthew 6:9–13, authors' paraphrase)

Soul Talk

1. What makes discipleship to Jesus practical?
2. Which of the discipleship stories in this chapter do you especially relate to? Why?
3. Which of the biblical blunders have you struggled with?
4. What is an example of how participating in church has fostered your discipleship to Jesus?
5. How was your experience with using the Lord's Prayer like a pocket lighter?

Packing List for the R Stage

Venturing into Responsibilities in Ministry is an exciting new step in your journey with Jesus. Here's what you'll need to progress in this stage:

1. Readiness to use your spiritual gift(s)
2. Scriptures on your identity in Christ
3. A heart to serve others
4. Soul care ideas (so you don't burn out!)

5

The R Stage:
Responsibilities in Ministry

We grow when we use our gifts
to serve God and bless people.

He leads me in the paths of righteousness for His name's sake.

Psalm 23:3 NKJV

"Some people tell me I'm doing too much, but I love my job and my church needs me." Danielle smiles confidently. She's in her late twenties and works as a human resources director, leads the motel ministry to transients at her church, and serves in the church's youth group. "It's great to be part of something bigger than me!" she exclaims. "I'm growing in my skills, and I enjoy the people I'm working with. I feel respected and find meaning as I use the talents God has given me to serve in my church and community."

Danielle is thriving in the stage of Responsibilities in Ministry, using her people skills and leadership gifts to serve the Lord. We're all greatly blessed by people like her in the R Stage. Because of them our world is a much better place. They are many of the paid and volunteer workers in churches, nonprofits, schools, community centers, businesses, healthcare, and public service.

Characteristics of the R Stage

We began our Psalm 23 pilgrimage by putting confidence in Jesus as our Shepherd (the C in the CHRIST stages). Then, with the help of Bible teachers, we grazed in green pastures and drank in still waters to grow in grace (the H Stage). Now, in the R Stage of Responsibilities in Ministry, we're ready to share with others the blessings we've received, the lessons we've learned, and the gifts God has given us. *Ministry* here refers to any work we do "for his name's sake" (Ps. 23:3), whether paid or volunteer. Your ministry might be as a small group leader, church leader, missionary, life coach, spiritual director, 12-step sponsor, gardener, artist, musician, blogger, soul friend, parent, marketplace worker, or witness for Christ in any job. Any act of Christly kindness is a cup of water to the thirsty that brings God's great reward (Matt. 10:42).

This stage of CHRIST formation may begin as early as our teen years. Teresa of Jesus combines our H and R Stages in her second stage of spiritual formation and observes that we often "live many years in this upright and well-ordered way."[1] We've learned and grown in the H Stage, and now it's time to give back by loving and serving others. In the R Stage we enjoy being active and achieving in our areas of ministry or work. Like an athlete, we want to win, but it's for God and the church. We are *doers*. We roll up our sleeves and get busy, whether solo or on a team. John Wesley's rule of life expresses this stage well:

Do all the good you can,
By all the means you can . . .
In all the places you can . . .

94

To all the people you can,
As long as ever you can.[2]

The psychology behind all this R Stage doing is identity development. It's a season for discovering your gifts and using them in your church or community. Ministry to others is an honor, but it can also be anxious. We may get self-conscious and worry, *What if I fail? What are people thinking about me as I do this? Am I making a real difference?* To bolster our confidence in the R Stage, we take on the beliefs and values of Christian authority figures, experts, or friends, so our faith tends to be conventional or conformist (Prov. 22:6). Our need for bonding is so strong that even nonconformists at this stage incorporate the attitudes of their leaders and band together.[3] So it's natural to feel anxious or insecure when you're stepping out to serve God in new ways, but it's a red flag if you fall into an identity crisis of discouragement, role confusion, or propping up a false self.[4]

Another red flag for slowing down our activism in the R Stage is if our need to be productive or serve God pulls us into giving too much, getting stressed out, or people-pleasing. We may become like the prodigal son's older brother, putting guilt on ourselves and others to *do more and do it better for God* (Luke 15:28–30). We become sick and tired (often literally) of being so dutiful, giving so much to others, and not being appreciated. Resentment builds. Cynicism strangles faith. We burn out. That's how driving a hundred miles an hour in the R Stage crashes us into The Wall!

An important part of the picture is that local churches draw attenders into the R Stage to serve and keep serving in order to meet the needs of the church, city, and world. It's similar with other Christian organizations or causes. The good side of this is that it encourages us to look beyond ourselves to care for others. The danger is that it can put pressure on us to overwork or over-program our lives. The stark reality is that *organizations tend to eat*

95

the souls of their servants—even if they're led by Christ-honoring and compassionate people. If you're a leader of others, you can diminish this risk by putting high priority on soul care for yourself and those you serve.

People in the R Stage say things like:

- "I feel a sense of identity as I serve with people like me. I've found that I'm actually good at this role!"
- "For me college isn't just about my studies—I serve on the student council, help in the outreach to refugees every week, and volunteer in the high school ministry at church."
- "I enjoy using my leadership gifts for our church ministries to the poor and needy in our city."
- "I have a passion for people scattered outside the organized church. I bring the Kingdom of God to them in the marketplace and neighborhood."
- "Failure is not an option for me. I'll do whatever it takes to succeed in what the Lord has called me to do."
- "Al-Anon helped me recover my family and faith. Giving back to others as a sponsor is the most important part of my week."
- "As a volunteer leader I'm blessed to have a great lead pastor to learn from."
- "I thought if I gave my free time to three different church ministries that God would take care of my family, but my wife became an alcoholic and our son is estranged from us."

Path Finder for the R Stage

For each statement below, circle T if it is true of your current experience with God.

YOUR CURRENT EXPERIENCE WITH GOD	TRUE?
1. Serving Christ with my gifts in church or ministry is my primary focus.	T
2. I strive to help others and serve the Lord.	T
3. I work for God but struggle to enjoy being with God as I work.	T
4. I tend to rely on my own abilities in what I do for God.	T
5. I believe my faith in God makes me more successful.	T
6. Often I get tired from serving in my church or ministry.	T
7. I have trouble setting limits on the ministry or service I offer.	T
8. Quiet prayer may be helpful, but it feels unproductive to me.	T

If you circled "true" more often for the R Stage than the other CHRIST stages, this may be your current home stage.

Roadblock: False Identity

The apostle John describes three temptations we need to overcome: "wanting your own way," "wanting everything for yourself," and "wanting to appear important" (1 John 2:16 MSG). Each sinful desire can become a false identity message:

- "You are what you do."
- "You are what you have."
- "You are what people say about you."

Becoming identified with these worldly wants generates the Cycle of Works and diminishes our service to God, especially at the R Stage. They're lies that reject God's love. We overcome them as we follow Jesus, who defeated Satan's lies in the wilderness by reciting truths from Scripture (Matt. 4:4, 7, 10). He refused a self-made-ego identity in favor of replenishing himself in his true-beloved-by-Abba self (Matt. 3:13–17).

John had his own identity challenges to work through. First, he may have felt he'd failed his father by not continuing in their fishing business (Matt. 4:22). Then he failed his Rabbi with disbelief, pride, ambition, and thundering anger (see Mark 10:35–45; Luke 9:54). Even as an apostle, he was always lost in the shadows of Peter and Paul.⁵ But John's career failures helped him succeed in his spiritual formation in Christ, which is what the Lord most wants from our life. John grew to be joyfully confident in his identity as "the disciple Jesus loves."⁶ The Beloved Disciple shows us that it's by abiding in Jesus' ministry of the Father's love for us that we love others well (John 15:5–12).

When I (Bill) was in my late twenties and in the R Stage, the Lord showed me that I was basing my identity on the lie of "you are what you do" rather than on Jesus' love for me. The lesson came at a time when I was embarrassed because I had a PhD in psychology but was working as a security guard. While I was completing my degree, I had been building my counseling practice. But after I graduated, my client load dropped from fifteen a week down to three, and new referrals were not coming in. I had spent eight years and over $100,000 on my education, and instead of being a doctor of the soul, I was a lowly doctor of security! I kept praying for God to bring me new clients, but no provision came. It felt like I'd wasted all that money and all those years of training. It seemed that my commitment to Christ wasn't blessing me as it had before. *I was in a desolation of feeling God's absence.*

One day I was mindlessly watching the security cameras when suddenly I sensed Christ speak to my heart: "Bill, why are you anxious and discouraged? Don't look to your PhD, your income, or what people think of you for your identity—learn to find your significance in me. Hold your head high because you belong to me!" Since then I've been setting aside my ego self to strengthen my true self in God's grace by repeating to myself John's affirmation that I'm a beloved disciple of Jesus. I've especially found it helpful to skip while exclaiming over and over, "I'm the disciple Jesus loves! I'm the disciple Jesus loves! I'm the disciple Jesus loves!" Try it. I bet you can't do it without smiling, if not laughing! You'll be surprised by how the grace and joy of Jesus gets into your body and personality.

Grace: Joy Gifts for Serving God

For many years as a mother of young children I (Kristi) was in the Responsibilities in Ministry stage. I balanced caring for our three children with being a therapist in private practice and volunteering in church, where I served in MOPS (Mothers of Preschoolers). Also, Bill and I helped start our church's Homebuilders ministry to young families, and our family went on multiple four-day mission trips to build houses for the poor in Mexico. Whenever I started serving in a new ministry, I felt overwhelmed and lacking in confidence. It was like the first time I was pregnant: I was afraid I might not feel love for my baby. How could I handle the responsibilities of motherhood if I didn't feel love in my heart? But I found that simply taking care of my child bonded us. In the same way, *our love for people and the joy of helping grow as we serve.*

I enjoyed consolation from God by ministering in the areas that interested me and related to my family and spiritual growth. I was blessed to make new friends and belong in community. I was helping young moms and other people grow in their discipleship to Jesus, and this was furthering my own growth because I needed to depend on Christ strengthening me and I was rubbing shoulders with other Christian leaders.

It may surprise you that Paul says it is "an honorable ambition" for us "to aspire to leadership" (1 Tim. 3:1 NEB). He urges us to "fan into flame the gift of God" (2 Tim. 1:6). You may not think of ambition and fiery work as godly traits, but as expressions of servant leadership they are. Moses was one of the greatest leaders in history and the Lord called him "my Servant" (Josh. 1:2). In fact, the word "leader" is only used six times in the Bible, but the word "servant" occurs 885 times! Servant leadership is the heart of Responsibilities in Ministry.

Personality tests like the Myers-Briggs, DISC, and Strengths-Finder give you different lenses for understanding how your Creator has endowed you for living and serving in the Kingdom of God.

Understanding and implementing our gifts and passions helps us to be more effective in our work and ministry. Your spiritual gifts are needed by others in the body of Christ, even as you need their gifts, so that everyone can share in God's work (Eph. 4:12). Whatever your work, the purpose is loving people by doing your best. "God honors the shoemaker's work not because he puts little crosses on his shoes but because he appreciates craftsmanship."[7]

Serving others with the talents God has given us fosters joy and healthy identity. For this reason, we call spiritual gifts *joy gifts*. We've put some fresh and practical wording to the ministry gifts listed in Romans 12:3–8 and Ephesians 4:11–13.[8] We hope this list helps you to hear or confirm God's call on your life. Which of the joy gifts in the table below do you have? What are the main gifts God has imparted to you for blessing others? Rank your top four gifts. (You may want to ask some friends how they experience you.)

Joy Gifts		
SPIRITUAL GIFT	DEFINITION	RANK
Dream-awakener	Starting new churches, ministries, or other works	
Truth-teller	Offering knowledge and wisdom for today's culture	
Includer	Wooing people to follow Jesus in a community	
Shepherd	Caring for the spiritual and personal needs of others	
Teacher	Showing people how to apply the Bible to their daily life	
Servant	Meeting practical needs for people	
Encourager	Inspiring strugglers to help them maximize their potential	
Investor	Donating money to expand the Kingdom of God and bless people	
Leader	Guiding people to follow Jesus in a specific way	
Healer	Giving mercy, empathy, and prayer to restore the sick or hurting	

Waiting for Your Opportunity

For some people in the R Stage, their identity is damaged because other leaders hold them back from being able to use their gifts. This roadblock is more likely to happen to women, minority ethnic groups, younger adults, and people who are creatives or feelers. Our friend Stacy was kept under a leadership lid in her church. She and her husband wanted to lead a small group in their Bible church with her as the teacher, but they were told she couldn't lead a group with men in it. (Would they say that to the many women leaders in the Bible like Deborah, Esther, Anna, the Virgin Mary, Mary Magdalene, Priscilla, and Junia?) Stacy had a Bible college degree, served as an ordained minister on the executive team in a Christian nonprofit, was a very gifted Bible teacher, and was known as a godly person, but the elders did not allow women to serve in leadership positions. She felt hurt and disrespected. She and her husband found another church home where they could lead a small group.[9]

Another challenge is that for many Christ-followers it can take a decade or more of adulthood before they begin to home in on using their best gifts in their work or ministry. They may feel like they're not fully released by the Lord into their passion and the real contribution of their life until they're in their forties or older and in the S Stage. As we'll be discussing in the next chapter, to experience the anointing and fruitfulness of Spirit-Led Ministry we usually have to go through The Wall and the stage of the Inner Journey. We need to mature in authentic faith through questioning our faith, disagreeing with our teachers, learning from failure, enduring suffering or spiritual dryness, and being faithful in hidden years of quietly serving God in the Little Way.

You may feel like the servant in Jesus' parable of the talents to whom the master gave the fewest talents. If you feel competitive or envious, that probably comes from feeling insignificant. You need empathy and to find self-esteem in being loved unconditionally. Then you need encouragement to invest what you have in the

Kingdom of God, even if it's in small or hidden ways. That's how you receive more talents to work with and get to revel in hearing the Master affirm, "Well done, good and faithful servant!" (Matt. 25:14–30).

We can draw positive motivation from anticipating the day of judgment in heaven when Christ the Righteous Judge has a crown of righteousness to award to *all* who love and serve him (2 Cor. 5:10; 2 Tim. 4:8). Many who seem the greatest now will be least in heaven (Matt. 19:30). Whatever our age or stage, we can find blessings in following the example of our Lord Jesus who worked as a common laborer until he was thirty years old, and then even during his public ministry he washed dirty feet and cooked breakfast for his hungry friends (John 13:14–15; 21:12).

Finding Your Rhythm

It was a hard and long season when I (Kristi) was in the R Stage and juggling the balls of responsibility that went with being a mother, wife, therapist, and helper in church. One day I was on retreat and the leader challenged us to spend five hours alone in solitude and silence with Jesus. Five hours seemed like a long time to be quiet and alone. I didn't know what to do, so I just started walking toward a creek that was nearby. I realized, *I don't even know what pace to walk!* It felt so weird because I was used to trying to walk really fast to keep up with Bill and his long legs, or to walk really slow and guide my kids along by the hand. Here I was free of everybody else's needs and wants and feelings, and it was like I almost didn't even know how to walk. I prayed, "Jesus, I don't know what my pace is. I don't know how to be myself!"

I was orbiting around other people and pleasing them. I would look to what they needed and care for them. I was trying to love people for Jesus, but I was exhausted! As I kept walking in the high altitude of the mountains, I got tired and a little queasy. This matched how I felt about the burdens I was carrying.

The Holy Spirit drew my mind to Jesus' words in Matthew 11: "Are you weary and worn out? Come to me and step into my yoke with me. Learn from me for I am gentle and humble of heart and you will find rest for your soul" (vv. 28–30, authors' paraphrase).

I started crying and arguing with Jesus. "No! What do you mean? Your yoke isn't easy—it's hard and heavy, and I'm worn out from trying to please you. I'm loving other people to serve you, and it's drained the life out of me."

I sensed Jesus replying, "Well, Kristi, you think my yoke is heavy because you think it's like Bill's yoke, and his yoke would be heavy for you—just as your yoke would be heavy for him. I have a yoke that's perfectly fit to you; it's perfectly sized for your personality and needs. If you'll learn to trust me and keep company with me and walk with me, like you're doing now, then you'll discover that *my yoke is restful for your soul.*"

Many of us in the stage of Responsibilities in Ministry are prone to people-please and miss Jesus' easy yoke of the "unforced rhythms of grace" (Matt. 11:29 MSG). Instead of trying to secure ourselves with other people's approval we need to seek first God's kingdom and righteousness and find our security in him (Matt. 6:33–34). Making people happy all the time and avoiding conflict with them are unhealthy spiritual formations that perpetuate a false self and diminish our ability to love others well. Instead, trusting God includes speaking the truth in love to people and resolving conflicts to foster unity (Eph. 4:15).[10]

Shining Your Light

My (Bill's) Grandpa B thrived in the R Stage. He is one of my faith heroes, but as a boy I was scared of him. He was a square-jawed, straight-eyed man with a stocky frame who liked to argue and always got his way. He epitomized Chicago as the hardworking City of Broad Shoulders. He played football at Illinois University with Red Grange, one of the greatest athletes in history, and he was a first alternate sprinter for the USA Olympic team in 1932. As an executive for Wisconsin Steel in Chicago, he negotiated against the labor unions for twenty years and *never lost*. When he had something to say, everyone listened. When he wanted something done, everyone jumped into action.

When he retired at age sixty-two, Grandpa B became a Christian. I was amazed to see the change in his personality—he became increasingly friendly, humble, and caring. He completed the Campus Crusade for Christ (now called CRU) training in evangelism. His faith in God was bold, compassionate, and unfailing. He'd strike up conversations with people everywhere he went and guide them through the Four Spiritual Laws because he wanted everyone to know the love of Christ. He had the greatest success at the hospital in downtown Chicago. Three times a week he visited there and told people, "I want to share with you the good news about Jesus Christ. Let's talk and I'll pray for you." In twenty-five years of ministry he led 65,000 people to Christ! For each person he wrote down their name and contact information and CRU sent follow-up discipleship materials.

Grandpa B shined his light for Christ. That's what we get to do in the R Stage. God created us to govern the creation; it's part of God's image in us to make distinct contributions that help people in our world (Gen. 1:26–28). Furthermore, Jesus Christ has given you a special light to shine that is very much needed by the people in your circle of influence (Matt. 5:14–16). *No one else has your uniquely God-created, Christ-redeemed, and Spirit-infused personality!*

I don't believe Grandpa B went beyond the R Stage, which illustrates that the stage we reach does not necessarily correlate with greater faith and fruitfulness—the measure of our life is love (Mark 12:30–31). Whatever our current CHRIST stage, we need to resist Satan's temptations to judge ourselves (or others) and entrust ourselves to God's grace. Brennan Manning shared a story to help us avoid the pitfalls of guilt and shame:

A prosecutor presented all of the sins of commission and omission that I was responsible for throughout my life. . . . That went on for hours, and it fell on me like a landslide. I was feeling worse and worse to the point where the soles of my feet were hot. . . . A group of angels appeared to conduct my defense. All they could say was, "But he loved." They began chanting this over and over again in a chorus: "But he loved. But he loved. But he loved." This continued until dawn, and in the end the angels won, and I was safe.[11]

Truly, Jesus' Great Commandment is a great relief! It's the bottom line of what God expects of us, and it's the best life. At each stage we're blessed to simply love God and share the love of Christ with the people around us (Mark 12:30–31).

Elijah's Disciplines

For the last decade we've brought our Soul Shepherding Institute to a network of over forty church-planting pastoral couples in Mexico. They live in very small and simple houses with no running water, work fifty hours a week as laborers earning two or three dollars an hour, and pastor in the evenings and on weekends. Recently, one of the young pastors in the R Stage was suffering from compassion fatigue. In his church of 150 people there were seven who were suicidal. His shoulders were slumped from the heavy burdens he'd been carrying. His brow was furrowed and his eyes flitted back and forth with worry. He was in danger of burnout. Our days together were timely for him and his wife to be poured into with empathy, affirmation, soul training, and prayer. By the end of the retreat his face had brightened, his shoulders were back, he was holding his wife's hand, and he had a strategy to bring back to his church.

Elijah's story in the Bible illustrates the danger of burnout and our need for soul care in the R Stage. He had three amazing accomplishments in quick succession: he defeated 450 false prophets of Baal by calling down fire from heaven, he prayed for rain and ended a three-year drought, and he raced a chariot in a twenty-mile marathon and won! He was at the peak of his ministry success and proud; he was basing his identity on his results rather than his relationship with Yahweh. Then the wicked queen Jezebel sent armies to kill him, and he hid trembling alone in the wilderness. In anger he judged the other prophets of Yahweh as inferior. In self-pity he complained that he was the only true prophet left. He became so depressed that he prayed for the Lord to take his life. It was a dark desolation in which he felt abandoned by the God he had worked so hard to serve.

Elijah collapsed under a tree, wanting to die. He didn't realize that Yahweh was guiding him to rest quietly there. He took a long nap. Then he ate a big meal, took another long nap, and ate another big meal. Then he went for a long walk in the desert till he found shelter in a cave. Here he finally turned his loneliness into solitude by praying and listening for God's guidance. He needed to practice basic self-care. Dallas Willard liked to call these "Elijah's disciplines."[12]

The great prophet had been focused on big events and miracles, so in his cave of solitary prayer he expected God to come in power. But there was no revelation—not in an earthquake, not in a fire, not in a mighty wind. Elijah needed to be still and rest more. He needed to release his expectations and wait on God longer. Finally, once he was well rested and softhearted, he heard the Lord Almighty speak in a gentle whisper. The Spirit told him that in fact he was *not* alone—there were seven thousand faithful servants in Israel. Furthermore, the Lord was giving him Elisha to train up so he could take over the ministry (1 Kings 18:16–19:18).

Like Elijah, in our service for God we may overwork, try too hard to meet everybody's needs, or neglect basic self-care. We're especially prone to this burnout path in the R Stage. Does this describe your life? As a leader or helper are you needing to attend to your needs? Which of Elijah's disciplines might help you enjoy life with Jesus in the Father's world?

- Getting more sleep
- Eating healthy
- Appreciating nature
- Receiving physical touches of comfort
- Exercising
- Talking honestly with God
- Being quiet and still
- Delegating tasks to others who have bandwidth

We'll learn more about Elijah's disciplines when we discuss The Wall in the next chapter.

Trail Markers for the R Stage

AGE	13 to adult
FAITH	Serving others with your gifts
COGNITIVE DEVELOPMENT	Conventional, identifying with authority
ROADBLOCK & TEMPTATIONS	False identity that damages self-esteem
	Overworking and relying on yourself rather than God
	Repressing personal desires and needs
	Judging yourself or others (e.g., shame or blame)
	Idealizing yourself or others
	Jealousy and selfish ambition
	Neglecting intimacy with God and soul care
IMAGE OF GOD	Lord and Master
GRACE	Joy gifts for serving God
LESSONS	Discovering your unique gifts to serve the Lord
	Taking on new responsibilities to help people in Jesus' name
	Improving productivity in your work/ministry for God
	Enjoying when God uses you to bless other people
	Caring for your relationship with God and your well-being
	Persevering with faith through the stress of ministry
SPIRITUAL DISCIPLINES	Service projects
	Expressing spiritual gifts and personality
	Books and classes on serving and leading
	Discovering identity in Christ
	Sharing the gospel
	Praying for others
	Giving and tithing
	Short-term mission trips
	Serving with a ministry leader
	Setting boundaries to not overwork
	Caring for your body (as Christ's temple)
CHURCH MINISTRIES	Going on mission trips
	Leading small groups (with curriculum)
	Discipling others (in a program)
	Teaching Bible classes
	Preaching

··············· **Guidebook Scriptures for the R Stage** ···············

- **God affirms you through people:** "And that special gift of ministry you were given when the leaders of the church laid hands on you and prayed—keep that dusted off and in use" (1 Tim. 4:14 MSG).

- **Serving others is key to discipleship:** "The smallest act of giving or receiving makes you a true apprentice" (Matt. 10:42 MSG).

- **Getting started is a big step:** "Do not despise these small beginnings, for the LORD rejoices to see the work begin" (Zech. 4:10 NLT).

- **Partner with and trust God for results:** "God makes the seed grow. The one who plants and the one who waters work together with the same purpose. . . . For we are both God's workers" (1 Cor. 3:7–9 NLT).

- **Watch over your soul and your teaching:** "Give careful attention to your spiritual life and every cherished truth you teach, for living what you preach will then release even more abundant life inside you and to all those who listen to you" (1 Tim. 4:16 TPT).

- **The Spirit helps us persevere in serving:** "Whoever sows to please the Spirit, from the Spirit will reap eternal life. Let us not become weary in doing good, for at the proper time we will reap a harvest if we do not give up" (Gal. 6:8–9).

Soul Care Practice

Working with Christ

After some years of serving God in the stage of Responsibilities in Ministry, we run into the limits of our own strength and abilities, which (as we discuss in the next chapter) is often part of why we encounter The Wall. Instead of just working *for* God we can also learn to work *with* God. In the way we serve God we need to learn to transfer from the Cycle of Works to the Cycle of Grace. If we get this vision in the R Stage of the CHRIST journey, then it prepares us for the I Stage (Inner Journey) when we slow down our productivity to foster deeper intimacy with Jesus and the Father. That in turn prepares us for the S Stage when we'll return to greater productivity and loving ministry, like at the R Stage, but with a new capacity for serving God in the presence and power of the Holy Spirit rather than merely relying on our own strength and gifts.

Dallas Willard gives a great illustration of what it looks like for you to do your best in your work *and* trust the Spirit of Jesus with you to help you:

> Let's say I'm a plumber and I'm going to clean out someone's sewer. How will I do this as Jesus would do it? If you encounter difficulties with the people you're serving or with the pipe or the machinery,

you never fight that battle alone. You invoke the presence of God. You expect to see something happen that is not the result of you.

If you train yourself to thank God when those "coincidences" happen, you'll see them as patterns in your life. The crucial thing is to be attentive to God's hand, not to get locked into one-on-one thinking: *It's me and this pipe!* Never do that.

A person has to train [their self] to think, *Now is the time to rely on God and to praise him for the solution that will come to me.* That's called "life in God." Training brings you to the point where you don't have to say, "I have to pay attention!" You routinely think, *This is an occasion when God is present. This is a time to pray, to praise.*[13]

What has happened for this plumber? God has helped him solve his problem with the pipe, yes. But what is far more important is that he has become the kind of person who not only has trained to be a great plumber but also has learned to *pray and praise God while he works on broken pipes.* That is a big deal, because plumbing problems can lead even expert plumbers to be grumpy and irritable. Plumbers who are skilled in plumbing *and* in depending on the Spirit of Jesus with them will do the best work and have the happiest customers.

Throughout my life when I (Bill) have been fixing something or working on a difficult project, I have been fixated on the attitude, "It's me and this pipe, and I've got to succeed!" I'm thankful to be learning to be more like this plumber who does his work in Jesus' easy yoke. Learning to be more relaxed, relational, and prayerful while I work has made my work more enjoyable and effective.

Christ Goes Ahead of You

When Mary Magdalene and her friends went to visit Jesus' tomb, an angel proclaimed the good news, "He has risen! He is not here. . . . He is going ahead of you into Galilee. There you will see him, just as he told you" (Mark 16:6–7). *The risen Son of God also meets you today.*

Let's try a guided meditation exercise for appreciating Christ with us as we work:

- Imagine Jesus risen from the dead and radiating like the sun. See him large in stature, brightly lit, and smiling with love to you . . .
- Identify a particular work or ministry activity and imagine yourself in that situation.
- Slowly pray, "Christ is risen! He goes ahead of me into _____" (name your challenge or opportunity in the blank).
- Repeat this guided meditation for a while. Then while you're working recall it briefly as often as you can remember.

Soul Talk

1. Which of the false identities or lies have you struggled with: "I am what I do"; "I am what I have"; "I am what people say about me"?
2. How does it feel to identify yourself as the disciple Jesus loves? What helps you to live that way?
3. Which joy gift(s) do you most enjoy using to serve others? How does this feel for you?
4. Which is your favorite Guidebook Scripture for Responsibilities in Ministry? What encourages you about this passage?
5. What was your experience with doing the guided meditation of Christ going ahead of you?

Packing List for The Wall

We'd rather not encounter The Wall. But it's part of the journey of the soul and it offers surprising grace from God. Here's what you'll need to grow during this transition season:

1. Open-mindedness to your faith questions, doubts, or distress
2. Empathy from a friend or guide
3. Appreciation for Jesus on the cross
4. Psalms of lament

6

Transition:
Through The Wall

Spiritual dryness and getting stuck are
hidden opportunities for deeper growth and joy.

Yea, though I walk through the valley of the shadow of
death,
I will fear no evil; for You are with me.

Psalm 23:4 NKJV

"I can't feel God's presence," Darren lamented to me (Bill).
"My spiritual life is dry as dust." He was a mission worker
with a warm and positive personality who served the Lord
faithfully. No one would've imagined that his soul tank was empty
and he felt far from God.

A decade ago when he was in college Darren had a special experience of God's love during a prayer meeting with other leaders at an urban missions conference. He recalled, "I had a vision
of Jesus that warmed my heart. That's when I received my call."

The next few years he was on fire spiritually in the H Stage and kept growing in his devotion to Christ and his experience of the Spirit. Then in the R Stage he and his wife bought a house in a poor neighborhood in the inner city of Los Angeles and opened their doors to the diverse community. He liked to quote from Saint Benedict's sixth-century *Rule*: "Let all guests be received as Christ."[1] They turned their home into a ministry outpost, inviting neighbors over for meals, holding a weekly worship service, building and fixing things for people in their workshop, and providing temporary housing for abused women and the homeless.

Darren kept opening his heart to take in people's broken lives, but it was taking a toll on him. Daily Bible reading became sterile. Praying for people was like going through a long, laborious list. He felt he was in a never-ending desert, yet he kept trudging on. He was offering others the living waters of God's love while he lived off the splashback of their appreciation at being blessed through his ministry. He couldn't drink enough splashes and his soul dried up.

Characteristics of The Wall

We were going along well on the Psalm 23 path till we came to "the ravine as dark as death."[2] The cheerful green pastures have gone brown. The still waters have dried up. Frost has wilted our flowers. What was fruitful in our service to God has become barren. What had been working in our prayer life now fails us. It's like the Jews losing their temple and being left with only the Wailing Wall, where they tuck prayer notes in the cracks between the stones. At The Wall exhaustion, pain, grief, unanswered questions, doubt, discouragement, aloneness, or spiritual dryness seem to block our way to God.

In this dark trough of desolation we often judge ourselves and feel shame. Instead, we can find comfort and courage by taking hold of the word affirming God's unseen presence: "I will fear no evil, for you are with me" (Ps. 23:4). We need to keep renewing our hope that our Shepherd is leading us *through* the dark valley. Indeed, he will bring us into the blessings of feasting at his table in the highlands, receiving his anointing, and drinking from an overflowing cup. Then we will know that we have been pursued by his goodness and love *all the days of our life* (Ps. 23:4–6).

We're likely to encounter The Wall after we leave home (literally or symbolically) and at least once more later in life.[3] Recall the Beloved Disciple's perspective on our journey: early on we enjoy Jesus' forgiveness and the Father's love, then we run into a wall of testing in which we must learn to rely on the word of God, and finally we serve as a spiritual mother or father to bless others (1 John 2:12–14). This pivotal test of The Wall is in the middle of the CHRIST stages. It's a transition season, not a stage. *Either we deny our distress and stay busy in the R Stage or we process our pain and questions to develop a deeper and more authentic faith in the I Stage.* And remember, we might experience a roadblock of suffering or doubt at any stage, which may or may not take us to The Wall. (Most trials or desolations are not walls.) In other words, we may experience The Wall in any CHRIST stage or before putting faith in Christ.

"The Wall represents our will meeting God's will face to face," Hagberg and Guelich write. "We decide anew whether we are willing to surrender and let God direct our lives."[4] But surrender feels different now. In the C Stage we declared our yes to God's will and we were blessed. Then we kept upping our commitment in the H and R Stages, doing more spiritual disciplines and working harder to serve the Lord, and we were rewarded. But these steps don't work at The Wall. Here, trying harder will get you stuck. Here dryness, disorientation, or pain put relentless pressure on you to turn around on the CHRIST path and head back to the familiarity of earlier stages. It often feels like wasted years of wandering in the badlands. That's what it's like to surrender to God at The Wall. It's no wonder it's been said that most Christians do not experience the later stages of spiritual maturity.[5]

Our situation at The Wall is like the Chinese word for "crisis," which combines the characters for "danger" and "opportunity." As was the case for Jesus in the desert wilderness, demons are fighting us even as angels are ministering to us (Mark 1:12–13). Which side will prevail? The great danger is that Satan's attacks can derail your trust in Christ. The opportunity comes when, like Jacob, you wrestle in prayer and prevail to experience the Lord's blessing (Gen. 32:22–30). The Spirit of Truth is revealing your deeper brokenness and need for mercy in order to draw you closer to Christ (John 14:26; Rom. 8:26). If you keep verbalizing your faith struggles, submitting your will to God, and resisting the deceiver, then you will eventually break free and find that God is near (James 4:7–8).

To rest, seek empathy, and wait on God at The Wall usually does not feel like growth, but it really is. We may work through the issues of The Wall for years in the I Stage, peeling back the layers of the onion of our soul, as our tears forge a new path for intimacy with God. Maybe you relate to one of these people at The Wall:

- "It's been a painful journey for me the past four years. I've been lonely at a wall, but now I see and feel a better way of living."
- "Hearing other people share their faith struggles helps me learn about my story and keep seeking God."
- "I was taught that emotions can't be trusted. Learning to feel and accept my emotions opened me up to a new relationship with God."
- "For forty years I thought the R Stage was as far as the Christian life went, but now I see a new life on the other side of The Wall."

- "Three times I hit The Wall and bounced back into the R Stage. Now I'm on the path to the promised land."
- "My first wall came after growing up with empty religion. For over a decade I was in an unhealthy version of the H and R Stages before I was truly born again."
- "I'm thankful for my wall season because it put me on this deeper journey."

Six Types of Walls

If I (Kristi) need to go to the bathroom during the night, it's a long walk in the dark, and I'm prone to bump into furniture and walls. So I imagine a map of our bedroom. I see with my mind what I can't see with my eyes so I know where to walk. That's what we need in dark times at The Wall. It's like the Israelites of old getting through the Red Sea on dry ground by trusting and following Yahweh's unseen footprints (Ps. 77:19). They trusted the Lord as their Way Maker.

Often I have talked with people who are spiritually discouraged or stuck and don't know how to proceed in their journey with Jesus. When I introduce to them The Wall in the CHRIST stages map, the lights go on. Instead of feeling alone in desolation, they're encouraged to learn that others like Darren have also felt compassion fatigue or spiritual dryness. Instead of feeling lost, they get language to describe their experience. Instead of distrusting God, they begin to appreciate that the sovereign Lord has a good purpose of leading them into a season of transition from Responsibilities in Ministry to a new stage of faith and grace at the Inner Journey.

Once they get the big picture of their map, then we explore why they're at The Wall so they can find their way through it into spiritual renewal. You may relate to one or more of these six different wall experiences.

Six Types of Walls	
TYPE	CAUSE
1. Burnout	Overworking in your job or ministry
2. Spiritual burnout	Compulsive spirituality, compassion fatigue
3. Blowout	Moral failing
4. Personal crisis	Disease, family problem, grief, or depression
5. Faith crisis	Disbelief or cynicism
6. Dark Night of the Soul[6]	Ongoing spiritual dryness

After the Israelites got through the wall of the Red Sea, they had to deal with the walls of Jericho. Those walls went away not by fighting them or by ignoring them. That's what leads to a burnout, blowout, health problem, or getting stuck in cynicism. Instead the Israelites walked around the city seven times while praising Yahweh and praying—then the walls came crashing down (Josh. 6:15–16, 20). To walk along your wall is to explore it, ask questions, and understand your experience with the help of a guide. To praise God at The Wall is to appreciate that your Redeemer is doing a healing work in you. If you keep trusting the sovereign Lord, your wall will eventually fall and you will see the first gleam of dawn shining on your path ahead (Prov. 4:18).

Path Finder for The Wall

For each statement below, circle T if it's true of your current experience with God.

YOUR CURRENT EXPERIENCE WITH GOD	TRUE?
1. For a while I have not been feeling God's love like I used to.	T
2. I feel burned out on working hard at my job or in ministry to others.	T
3. I'm stuck in my spiritual life, like I've run into a wall.	T
4. I used to be more certain in my faith, but now I have questions and doubts.	T
5. I'm suffering with health or family problems and it seems God is not helping me.	T

YOUR CURRENT EXPERIENCE WITH GOD	TRUE?
6. I'm struggling to trust that God's purposes for me are good.	T
7. My spiritual practices are not blessing me like they did before.	T
8. If I pray quietly it brings up questions or distress.	T

If you circled three or more statements as true, you may be in a transition season at The Wall.

The Two Halves of Life

A woman we know was emotionally vulnerable with a church leader, who judged her as lacking faith and used Bible verses to justify his position. She was in the tender place of beginning the I Stage in the Second Half, and he had become hard-nosed in the R Stage in the First Half. The church's website featured rules for who may not take communion, why it's not good to drink alcohol, and why women are not allowed to serve as church leaders. That's like what the Pharisees did to people in Jesus' day, and it keeps people away from God's love (Matt. 23). Tragically, church history is full of religious bullies in the First Half who persecute people for wrong doctrine and yet remain blind to their own lack of mercy (Matt. 9:13). With a log of judgment in their own eye, they try to take a speck out of someone else's eye (Matt. 7:3–5).

We don't mean to imply that the spirituality of the Second Half is automatically better than that of the First Half, because that's not necessarily true. For example, a church leader in the S Stage of Spirit-Led Ministry recommended the books and podcasts of someone who promotes Christian universalism, and it confused a number of people in his church who were seeking to follow and serve Jesus in the First Half. One college student stopped attending church. When the leader was questioned about this, he defended himself by saying, "I'm not responsible for other people's faith and decisions." Actually, the Bible teaches us to be especially careful that we do not cause those who are newer or weaker in their faith to stumble (1 Cor. 8:9–13). Just venting negative judgments about a Christian speaker or church can damage those within earshot.

The two halves of life are like two different soul containers or spiritualities in which we have contrasting values, temptations, and strengths (see the table below).[7] From the First Half to the Second Half is such a momentous paradigm shift in our personality and faith that often there is misunderstanding, distrust, or strife between the two. In fact, we've observed this to be a major factor in church splits and family conflicts.

Before The Wall, in the C, H, and R Stages, our mindset is that life as a Christian should be fair, orderly, and safe, so we view things in black-and-white categories and we're earnest about doing everything right. In our spiritual disciplines and activities, we're prone to legalism, despite believing in God's grace. Then at The Wall our world is turned upside down by overwhelming personal struggle or failure. We come out the other side by resting in the empathy and mercy of Christ and abandoning ourselves to the Lord's sovereign will.

After The Wall, in the I, S, and T Stages, we step into a new world of universal compassion. We reorient to God's unfailing goodness and always-present love, become open to gray areas in life, and respond to psalms more than law.[8] Our focus has shifted from external behaviors to internal motives, from doing *for* God to being *with* God. Now our spiritual rhythms can be more relational, flexible, and integrated into our daily life. We're quicker to extend grace to everyone, especially those who are vulnerable or disadvantaged.

Both Halves Are Good

Stage theory can be misused to judge people, but we wrote this book to promote empathy and unity. Each CHRIST stage is good

TWO SPIRITUALITIES		
	FIRST HALF	**SECOND HALF**
STAGES OF FAITH	C, H, and R	I, S, and T
PURPOSE	Develop Christian identity and belonging	Practice a Christlike way of life
COGNITIVE FRAMEWORK	Black-and-white categories (dualistic) Seek decisions and results	Open to gray areas (both-and) Seek relational process
DANGERS	Judgmentalism and prejudice Closed-mindedness	Leaving church Diminishing the Bible
VALUES	Law Tradition and rules (authority) Security in God's blessings Outward behavior and image Productivity	Psalms (and poetry) Freedom, mercy for all Security in God's kingdom Inward character, heart Fruitfulness
EMOTIONAL HEALTH	Minimize emotions, react Avoid suffering	Give and receive empathy Learn from suffering
RESPONSE TO PERSONAL SIN	Feel guilty or righteous	Confession, forgiveness
DEVOTIONAL STYLE	Bible programs Prayer lists	Experiences with living Word Quiet prayer to rest in God
SOURCE OF MINISTRY	Own abilities, knowledge	Presence of Holy Spirit

in its time, and the value of our faith is not found in our stage but in our love for God and neighbor. When we're younger in age or spiritual maturity we need the security, clarity, orderliness, earning mentality, and sense of control that go with the First Half. Furthermore, organizations tend to rely on the First Half mentality, and like gravity, they pull us into these operating efficiencies. Productivity is not bad—it's a natural part of life at any stage, and it especially facilitates our growth in the early stages of grace. In fact, in this life we never totally leave the First Half. Even as Second Half apprentices to Jesus we will at times revisit aspects of earlier stages. As therapists we call this "regression in the service of growth." *Sometimes we need to go backward to go forward in a deeper or healthier way.* Remember, the CHRIST stages are not a linear progression—they're a spiral that's unique for each person.

However, if as adults we don't learn to accept the unsettling challenges of The Wall and the Spirit's invitation to cross over into the emotional honesty and deep love for Jesus and others that go with the Inner Journey, then problems start to mushroom in our character. We tend to become legalistic, closed-minded, defensive, judgmental, racist, sectarian, and hypocritical. Yet, we may not realize we're like that if we've unconsciously covered it all with a biblical theology of grace and an external moral formation. As in the old tale "The Emperor's New Clothes," other people can see our naked sin that we're denying.

It's natural to take a number of years in the spirituality of the First Half before taking on the attitudes and capacities of the Second Half, but *it's a problem if we get stuck in an earlier stage while serving in leadership.* This is one reason why the Bible specifically warns against newer Christ-followers being leaders (1 Tim. 3:6; James 3:1). As Paul makes clear, the point is not about chronological age but *spiritual maturity* (1 Tim. 4:12). What is spiritual maturity? First Half leaders may mistakenly think it's all about beliefs and behaviors, but close examination of the biblical qualifications for spiritual elders shows that some of the traits focus on emotional intelligence (EQ) and relational health.[9] Ultimately, leadership is about loving people.

On the other side, Second Half leaders may focus so much on inclusiveness that they lose the centrality of faith in Jesus Christ. But the New Testament clearly points to Jesus as *the* Way; he's our Mediator who reconciles us to God (John 14:6; 1 Tim. 2:5). Furthermore, they may unwittingly contradict the open-minded tolerance they espouse by disparaging earnest Bible adherents as "fundamentalists." They may devalue the law (or Christian doctrine), not realizing that when used rightly God's law is the structure of a life of grace (1 Tim. 1:8).

As you've seen so far, at each stage of the journey there are pitfalls and graces. Always our great opportunity is to apprentice ourselves to Jesus in the Kingdom of God by declaring, "My life is your school for teaching me. . . . In all things today I pray, 'Your will, your way, your time.' . . . Today, I look to love others as you love me."[10]

Roadblock: Distrusting God

At The Wall we're susceptible to distrust God because we feel we've outgrown what our parents, church, or other spiritual leaders taught us. We ask lots of questions and do our own thinking. We doubt or disagree with the beliefs, values, and traditions we once adhered to, and our faith may be left hanging in the air. On one hand, we need our parents and church leaders to give us space and grace to be emotionally honest and develop our own faith. On the other hand, if we're not careful, our emotional doubts and intellectual questions can harden into disbelief, cynicism, and isolation, cutting us off from the spiritual community and grace of God that we especially need at The Wall. Tragically, we may become resigned to a faith that lacks intimacy and vitality. Distancing from God is a slippery slope that may begin as innocuously as making a habit of choosing the beach, a golf course, or shopping over church and Christian community.

A research study by David Kinnaman, president of the Barna Group, found that 64 percent of eighteen- to twenty-nine-year-olds who had previously been active in church stopped attending.[11] This was a 10 percent increase from just eight years earlier. They left church because it seemed overprotective, shallow, antagonistic to science, judgmental of sex, intolerant of other views, and unfriendly to doubt.[12] In other words, they felt they needed more freedom for investigation and expression.

What about the young adults who stayed in church? How did they weather their faith storms? How did they deal with their disappointments, hurts, and stressors with church? They were termed "resilient disciples" and had four qualities of healthy faith that are vital at The Wall:

1. Personal relationship with Jesus Christ
2. Participating in Christian community
3. Valuing the Bible as inspired by God
4. Integrating their faith with the world[13]

The theme here is that the resilient Christ-followers took personal responsibility for their spiritual growth and relationships; they became *self-feeders* with God's grace, even in trials and experiences of desolation when God felt distant. Their growth in grace fueled their compassion for others.

Another large study that focused on adult church attenders found that 25 percent of them were either stalled in their spiritual life or dissatisfied with church. The researchers concluded that these strugglers needed coaching on how to use spiritual disciplines to resume their growth in Christ.[14] This is why we recommend particular soul training practices to fit each CHRIST stage. At The Wall, when the dry desolation can be overwhelming, the renewing disciplines involve rest, empathy, reflective prayer, and submitting to the sovereign Lord. When David was in trouble, these are ways that he strengthened himself in the Lord and "resouled"[15] (1 Sam. 30:6; 2 Sam. 16:14).

Leaning into The Wall

One time when I (Bill) was river rafting, our guide taught us, "If I yell, 'High water hard!' that means we're heading down into fast rapids. You have to *lean forward* into the high waters and paddle hard—or else we'll flip over. Especially if you're one of the front paddlers, we need you!" That got my attention because when waves are crashing into you the natural reaction is to lean back.

I was in the front of the raft because I like to be where the action is! When our guide yelled, "High water hard!" I was ready and leaned out over the tip of the raft into the splashing waves and paddled furiously. We navigated past jutting rocks, crashed through white-water turbulence splashing in our faces, and then dove down a five-foot waterfall. We made it, but our guide yelled out to his partner in the raft behind us, "Rescue!" One of the women on our raft forgot to lean forward and had been catapulted into the raging river. Fortunately, we were able to pull her out.

In life it's important to listen to our Guide's counterintuitive instruction to lean into turbulence. This is crucial for maintaining a healthy faith and participation in church and Christian community. Jesus' little brother urges us to accept our troubles and desolations as learning opportunities:

> Dear brothers [and sisters], is your life full of difficulties and temptations? Then be happy, for when the way is rough, your patience has a chance to grow. So let it grow, and don't try to squirm out of your problems. For when your patience is finally in full bloom, then you will be ready for anything, strong in character, full and complete. (James 1:2–4 TLB)

Happy patience in trials seems like a contradiction, especially at The Wall when we feel spiritually dry. But if we let ourselves feel our true thirst, then, like the Samaritan woman, we realize that more than being dry-mouthed we're *dry-souled* and *nothing but the Messiah's living waters will satisfy us* (John 4:13–15). This longing for God's love is what woos us into the Inner Journey stage of emotional honesty and intimacy with Jesus and fellow disciples. We get through the valley of the shadow of death by appreciating that our Shepherd-Lord is indeed with us (Ps. 23:4). We're learning to "walk by faith, not by sight" (2 Cor. 5:7 ESV). In time patience brings reward. As the Swiss psychoanalyst Carl Jung puts it, accepting "necessary suffering" now helps us prevent "unnecessary suffering" later.[16]

Grace: God's Empathy

C. S. Lewis had to learn to lean into The Wall and trust the empathy of Immanuel to meet him. When he was in his fifties he married Joy Davidman Gresham and experienced new joy and intimacy with God. He says they "feasted on love," and this was "sometimes as dramatic as thunderstorms, sometimes as comfortable . . . as putting on your soft slippers."[17] But after just four years of marriage, Joy died of cancer at age forty-five. This triggered Lewis' old grief of being a young boy and losing his mother to cancer. In his tearful despair he felt abandoned by God:

> When you are happy, so happy that you have no sense of needing [God] . . . if you remember yourself and turn to Him with gratitude and praise you will be—or so it feels—welcomed with open arms. But go to Him when your need is desperate, when all other help is in vain, and what do you find? A door slammed in your face, and a sound of bolting and double bolting on the inside. After that, silence. You may as well turn away. . . . There are no lights in the windows. It might be an empty house. Was it ever inhabited? It seemed so once. . . .
>
> The real danger is of coming to believe such dreadful things about [God]. The conclusion I dread is not, "So there's no God after all," but, "So this is what God's really like. Deceive yourself no longer."[18]

Lewis may have experienced what psychiatrist James Masterson calls "abandonment depression."[19] This profound sadness is often part of adult grief that goes back to early childhood traumas like losing a loved one, emotional neglect, abuse, or being hospitalized. Another example is when a toddler feels repeatedly punished by their mother (or other caregiver) for expressions of independence or anger, rather than receiving empathy and blessing. These early wounds tend to be experienced as a rejection and can have a depressing effect on personality. To know what early experiences shaped your story you may be able to supplement your memories by asking a parent or someone who knew you as a child. Also, you can infer your early developmental experiences from what you do remember of your childhood.

The psalmist offers us empathy in the pit of abandonment depression. For instance, Asaph prays, "Will the Lord reject forever? Will he never show his favor again?" (Ps. 77:7). Similarly, Job cries out to Yahweh from the pit when he suffers so much loss, pain, and injustice (Job 17:10–16). It was the same for Hagar when Sarah and Abraham sent her away (Gen. 21:14–16), for Naomi when her husband and two sons died (Ruth 1:21), and for Jonah when he was swallowed by a huge fish (Jon. 2:6). They all overcame a damaged image of God and the desolation of feeling alone to discover that even in the darkest valley their Shepherd-King was near.

C. S. Lewis wrestled with spiritual doubt and an image of God as distant. When he was a boy and God didn't heal his mother's cancer, he decided he didn't want to be a Christian anymore. In his early thirties he reconnected with God, but still he wrote to his friend Arthur Greeves, "Often when I pray, I wonder if I am not posting letters to a non-existent address."[20] But then he broke through from skepticism to a relationship with Christ that was increasingly personal and life-giving.[21] Twenty years later, when his beloved wife died so young, all his grief and distrust in God came back as he felt God had slammed the door in his face and left him alone on a cold, dark night.

But this time his faith was resurgent. He practiced his own teaching by accepting his pain as God's megaphone to rouse his soul.[22] He was courageous to keep venting his grief, doubt, fear, and anger to his friends as well as to God through praying the Psalms and journaling. He found comfort in the loving presence of the Crucified One, especially in the Eucharist. Then one day as he approached Christ in prayer, he saw a compassionate gaze and heard the sound of a chuckle, which seemed to say, "Peace child; you don't understand."[23] God's love broke through again.

Steps to Breakthrough

When I (Bill) ran the Boston Marathon a few years ago, many challenges came against me. First, my GPS watch broke and I ran too fast. Then the heat and humidity both rose into the 90s and runners were dropping from leg cramps, dehydration, and heat stroke. Then I had to run over hill after hill, culminating in the dreaded series of Heartbreak Hills on the last third of the race. Then I hit hard into The Wall that marathon runners dread: *I was exhausted, my legs were like lead, and I had shooting pains radiating up from my feet. I wanted to quit!* But I kept running till the finish line at 26.2 miles.

How did I do it? How did I get through The Wall and complete the marathon? I held on to Hebrews 12 in my heart:

> Therefore, since we are surrounded by such a great cloud of witnesses, let us throw off everything that hinders and the sin that so easily entangles. And let us run with perseverance the race marked out for us, fixing our eyes on Jesus, the pioneer and perfecter of faith. For the joy set before him he endured the cross, scorning its shame, and sat down at the right hand of the throne of God. Consider him who endured such opposition from sinners, so that you will not grow weary and lose heart. (vv. 1–3)

As I ran, I prayed this Scripture to myself over and over to fix my eyes on Jesus. I drew empathy and hope from my Lord: *He felt my fatigue and pain and he endured with joy to the finish line of his cross* (vv. 2–4). I also absorbed empathy and hope from the crowd of half a million people lining the streets of Boston. For literally every step of the 26.2 miles people kept clapping and shouting out, "You're doing great! You can do it!" They served up water, fruit, and energy bars for me. They sprayed me with water hoses. One person held out a sign with Hebrews 12:1–2 on it! These people were like Jesus' cloud of witnesses encouraging me (v. 1).

Kristi was in that crowd, and in the middle of the race she ran and gave me a hug and kiss. She helped me accept my limits and cast off the burden of expecting myself to finish the marathon in a fast time. I became content with running a slower pace, so I got through The Wall with Jesus and finished the race.

The opening of Hebrews 12 can serve as a general introduction to four practical steps that Darren took over some months to get through The Wall and into a new season of grace.

1. Fix Your Eyes on Jesus

Darren couldn't keep living off the splashback of his ministry to the poor in Los Angeles—he needed fresh wells of living water for his own soul. It was a big shift for him to realize that his first calling as a pastor was not to the people he served but to his own intimacy with Jesus. One way he drew closer to the Lord was to use our *Unforsaken* booklet as a guide through the Gospel stories of Jesus' sufferings on his cross-walk.[24] He was moved to tears and strengthened in his soul to see how Jesus' love relationship with his Father was the joy that sustained his sacrifice and suffering and empowered him to love everyone around him.

2. Ask for Empathy and Prayer

I asked Darren who was praying for him and his ministry. He replied, "I haven't asked anyone because I don't want to be needy and bother people. I'm responsible for myself." I challenged his thinking by explaining that even Jesus asked people to pray for him when he was in desolation (Matt. 26:36–41). Darren learned to ask for and appreciate listening and prayer from me and his friends. *When you're at The Wall it's the most important time in your journey with Jesus to seek support from a spiritual director or counselor.*

3. Find Hope

When Darren learned about the journey through the CHRIST stages, he was encouraged. "For years I kept slapping up against The Wall and felt like I was backsliding. I didn't understand. I never thought about Paul hitting a wall. It's such a relief to know this is normal and can spur my growth into a deep and joyful intimacy with God in the Inner Journey."

4. Unburden Yourself

To experience spiritual renewal, Darren needed to set boundaries on his ministry-aholic behavior and rigorous personal disciplines. He had compassion fatigue and was burned out on serving people in need and praying through lists of petitions. He had commitment fatigue and was burned out on Bible study and daily disciplines. He couldn't do it anymore and shut down. He needed to stop "should-ing" on himself and learn to rest in God's grace that frees us from shame.

"Do Nothing"

In Dallas Willard's two-week seminary class conducted at a monastery, he had me (Bill) and the other pastors take a twenty-four-hour silent retreat to rest and simply be with Jesus. His instructions were stark: "Do nothing. Don't try to make anything happen." There was a long, awkward silence. Then he repeated with a mischievous smile, "Do nothing. Don't try to make anything happen." *That was it.* Then he stepped away from the lectern, packed up his briefcase for the weekend, and walked out. As soon as we left the classroom our silence would begin.

A group of younger pastors who seemed overworked in the R Stage huddled together and called me over. They laughed nervously, "Bill, you lead silent retreats for pastors—help!"

"This is a new challenge for you," I empathized. "I understand why you feel anxious about it."

"But what can we *do*?" asked one of them.

I replied, "Probably *we need to do something in order to do nothing.*" I suggested, "You could take a prayer walk. Or just take a nap—Jesus took naps. Try meditating on a Scripture till you fall asleep."

One of the guys joked sarcastically, "But we're not going to sleep for the whole weekend of silence!"

"I know it's tough," I replied. "If you keep doing nothing, your body will be jittery, your thoughts will wander, and you'll feel pressure to be productive. But if you stay with it, then you'll feel *bored*—that's when you know the solitude and silence are working and you can practice resting in God's arms of grace and listening." Then I briefly taught them how to relax in God's presence with a breath prayer from the Bible (like we did at the end of chapter 3).

After I left the classroom I bumped into Dallas in the hallway and he whispered, "Are you going out on the mountain?"

I replied in earnest, "No. I think I'll just sit still in my room and contemplate."

He tilted his head. "Why would you do *that*? You can find solitude on the mountain and I know you love to hike." As usual, he pegged me: I was being overly ascetic. I gave Dallas a hug. Then, like a deer, I bounded out for a hike with Jesus!

When I (Kristi) was at The Wall, one of my do-nothing disciplines was to float on a raft in the ocean while meditating on 1 Corinthians 13. I don't like cold water or rough waves, and I'm afraid of sharks and jellyfish. But I ventured into the ocean and lay down on my raft to express my trust in God's love to hold me and keep me safe. Then I prayed each verse on God's perfect love into my trials and for people I was concerned about. This nurtured Inner Journey spirituality for me.

When people at The Wall hear the typical spiritual growth advice to read the Bible more, pray more, serve others more, and try harder to be like Jesus, they often have an *allergic reaction* of shutting down or getting angry. They need the freedom to do nothing *with Jesus*. The passageway through The Wall is to "make every effort to enter [God's] rest," opening our hearts to the loving words of God and to one another (Heb. 4:11–13).

If we don't *choose* to rest, then we'll probably be *forced* to do so by sickness or another crisis. It's like a pell-mell sheep, reckless and scattered and putting itself and the flock in danger, may need the shepherd to break its legs and carry it. It's a *severe mercy*. Sometimes an experience of spiritual desolation proves to be a great grace.

Are you tired? Spiritually frustrated? Feeling stuck at The Wall? Don't try to push through this or distract yourself. It's time to stop *doing for* the Lord and start *being with* the Lord. Look to Jesus on the cross and see that God has torn down the veil in the temple that kept us at a distance (Matt. 27:51).

Holy Idleness

As we're writing this, we're in quarantine from the COVID-19 pandemic. It seems our whole world, including the Church, is at The Wall. We're stuck in a place of fear over sickness and riots and racial tensions and politics. We're overwhelmed with mental health issues as alcohol abuse, domestic violence, and suicides have surged. Divorce rates are also skyrocketing, especially among newlyweds. What has happened to us?

One explanation is Blaise Pascal's incisive observation from centuries ago: "The sole cause of people's unhappiness is that they do not know how to stay quietly in their own room."[25] People who know how to be alone and quiet for a long time, to simply rest in God's unconditional love without having to accomplish anything or be entertained, are much better able to be at peace in a crisis and bless those who curse them.

John of the Cross, a sixteenth-century Spanish priest and a friend of Teresa's, is a shining example. As we'll discuss in chapter 8, he experienced intense religious persecution and was kept in solitary confinement for nearly a year. During his imprisonment, he kept a loving vigil with Jesus at the cross and extended blessings to his captors. Prior to this trial, John had learned to practice "holy idleness." He challenges pastors and Christian workers, insisting "that they would profit their church and please God much more . . . were they to spend at least half of this time with God in prayer."[26] Cutting your work in half? For most of us that feels impossible! The crucial point at The Wall is to put Sabbath rest before doing our work.[27]

At first practicing holy idleness may make us jittery and distressed as we learn to deal with negative emotions we've been denying. But if we stay with it, we can learn to feel loved by God, rested, and rejuvenated. Even Winnie the Pooh quipped, "Doing nothing often leads to the very best something!"[28]

Here are examples of do-nothing disciplines that can help us to rest, recuperate, and realign ourselves for a soul pivot from The Wall to the Inner Journey (I Stage) with Jesus:

- Take a nap as you imagine laying your head on Jesus' chest like John did (John 13:23).
- Seek empathy from a soul friend.
- Read, listen to, or watch a story of someone following Christ through trials.
- Ask God to lead you as you walk, jog, hike, bike, or drive without having a destination in mind. (Being active physically can help us to be still spiritually.)
- Play music, draw a picture, or write a poem and offer it as a prayer.
- Enjoy a fun activity with Jesus! (A pastor in our Institute spent her solitude day at Disneyland.)
- Pray a psalm that expresses your distress (see the soul care practice below).

Trail Markers for The Wall

AGE	18+ (especially midlife)
FAITH	Hope and submission to God
COGNITIVE DEVELOPMENT	Questioning authority and norms; open-minded
ROADBLOCK & TEMPTATIONS	Distrusting God (may become cynicism)
	Self-will, stubbornness
	Blaming yourself (shame)
	Leaving home or family values in an angry way
	Not attending church
	Going through the motions of faith
	Escaping distress in diversions
	Regressing to an earlier stage
IMAGE OF GOD	Jesus on the cross and the sovereign Lord
GRACE	God's empathy for your distress
LESSONS	Trusting God's will for you is good (even when it feels bad)
	Admitting your distress, doubts, questions, or resistance
	Dismantling your ego self to build a new self in Christ
	Continuing to rest in God's grace even if it feels flat
	Trying new ways to pray and read Scripture
	Cultivating new motivation to love the Lord
SPIRITUAL DISCIPLINES	Receiving spiritual care or counseling
	Setting boundaries (to do less work or ministry)
	Enjoying God's blessings in nature, friends, and the arts
	Taking a nap while meditating on Scripture
	Praying Psalms of lament (and journaling)
	Stations of the Cross
	Studying the CHRIST stages of faith
	Reading stories of people growing through faith trials
	Retreats (especially with solitude and silence)
	Prayer walks in a labyrinth
	Prayer of relinquishment
	Visual devotions (picture prayers)[29]
CHURCH MINISTRIES	Serving the poor and needy
	Creative arts

·············· **Guidebook Scriptures for The Wall** ···············

- **There's a hidden blessing in trials:** "We know that suffering produces perseverance; perseverance, character; and character, hope" (Rom. 5:3–4).
- **The Wall is temporary:** "With my God I can scale a wall" (Ps. 18:29).
- **Rest and refresh with Jesus:** "But so many people were coming and going that Jesus and the apostles did not even have a chance to eat. Then Jesus said, 'Let's go to a place where we can be alone and get some rest'" (Mark 6:31 CEV).
- **Faith wrestles through emotional struggles:** "How long, LORD? Will you forget me forever? How long will you hide your face from me? How long must I wrestle with my thoughts and day after day have sorrow in my heart? How long will my enemy triumph over me?" (Ps. 13:1–2).
- **Empathy facilitates submission to God's will:** "'Abba, Father,' [Jesus] cried out, 'everything is possible for you. Please take this cup of suffering away from me. Yet I want your will to be done, not mine'" (Mark 14:36 NLT).
- **Ask God to help your unbelief:** "Immediately the father of the [sick] child cried out and said with tears, 'Lord, I believe; help my unbelief!'" (Mark 9:24 NKJV).
- **Keep hoping—God's blessing is coming!** "Be alert, be present. I'm about to do something brand-new. It's bursting out! Don't you see it? There it is! I'm making a road through the desert, rivers in the badlands" (Isa. 43:19 MSG).

Soul Care Practice

Praying a Psalm of Lament

In Psalm 22 we see a prophetic image of Jesus at The Wall. He's hanging naked on the cross, disfigured from beatings, bleeding profusely, suffocating to death, and bearing our sin and shame. The Man of Sorrows cries out for all to hear, "My God, my God, why have you forsaken me?" (Ps. 22:1). It's the only time Jesus doesn't call God "Father."

But there's more. Often we read only the first verse of Psalm 22 and don't realize that Jesus verbalized that as a *remez* to invoke the whole Psalm, which at that time included Psalm 23.[30] This means that on the cross Jesus also prayed, "[God] has not hidden his face from [me] . . . but has listened to [my] cry for help" (Ps. 22:24) and "The LORD is my shepherd; I shall not want" (Ps. 23:1 NKJV). This suggests that Jesus *felt* forsaken by God on the cross but was not actually abandoned. God the Father does not abandon his Son, and he won't abandon you (Mark 14:36).[31]

The affirmations of Psalm 23 that Jesus received on the cross are for you in your trial. At The Wall you probably feel that it's your fault or that God has rejected you. But you can pray with Jesus, "[Father God] is my shepherd, I lack nothing. . . . Even though I walk through the darkest valley, I will fear no evil, *for you are with me*" (vv. 1, 4, emphasis added).

Psalms 22 and 23 give language for the disorientation and distress we feel at The Wall (and in other trials) and inspire our prayers of faith so we can reorient to the loving presence of our Shepherd-Christ.[32] "His wounds [become] your healing" (1 Pet. 2:24 MSG).

Psalms 22–23 Meditation

Jesus prepared for his cross with a "watch and pray" discipline in the Garden of Gethsemane. He anticipated the cross in prayer before he endured the whips and was nailed to the wood. The emotionally honest and submissive way he prayed in the shadow of the cross is how he prayed while hanging on the cross (Matt. 26:36–44). He's showing us how to train ourselves to trust in God so that we can endure our cross with courage and joyful anticipation of resurrection. (Recall our discussion in chapter 3 of Peter learning to watch and pray so God could heal his soul split.)

Here are some steps to watch and pray with Jesus:

1. Identify a personal trial and offer it to the Lord.
2. Imagine Jesus on the cross loving you.
3. Pray these verses of Psalms 22 and 23:

   "Why are you so far from saving me, so far from my cries of anguish? My God, I cry out by day, but you do not answer, by night, but I find no rest" (22:1–2).

   "I am a worm and not a [person], scorned by everyone, despised by the people" (22:6).

   "I am poured out like water, and all my bones are out of joint" (22:14).

   "But you, Lord, do not be far from me. You are my strength; come quickly to help me" (22:19).

"For [the LORD] has not despised or scorned the suffering of the afflicted one; he has not hidden his face from him but has listened to his cry for help" (22:24).

"The LORD is my shepherd, I lack nothing. . . . Even though I walk through the darkest valley, I will fear no evil, for you are with me" (23:1, 4).

"Surely your goodness and love will follow me all the days of my life, and I will dwell in the house of the LORD forever" (23:6).

4. In your own words talk to Jesus about how you're feeling in your trial.

5. Go back to the words of the psalms above and underline God's promises to you.

Soul Talk

1. How is it helpful for you to understand The Wall as a transition season from the First Half to the Second Half of the CHRIST stages?

2. Which of the six types of walls have you or someone close to you encountered (burnout, compassion fatigue, moral blowout, personal crisis, faith crisis, Dark Night of feeling far from God)? Briefly describe this.

3. Who in the Bible encourages you that you can break through tough times? How do you relate to their story?

4. What is one Guidebook Scripture on The Wall that is helpful to you? Why?

5. What was your experience praying Psalms 22 and 23 with Jesus for your trial?

Packing List for the I Stage

The Inner Journey features a spiritual renewal of enjoying God's love. To grow deeper in this stage you'll need:

1. Acceptance of your emotions and needs
2. Dependence on the Spirit to cultivate intimacy with Jesus and his Abba
3. Longing for God's presence
4. Quiet prayer

The I Stage:
Inner Journey

We experience spiritual renewal through empathy, emotional growth, and longing for God.

> Your rod and Your staff, they comfort me.
> You prepare a table before me in the presence of my enemies.
>
> Psalm 23:4–5 NKJV

In my thirties I (Kristi) was in the R Stage and felt like I was growing in my faith. During that time Bill and I attended a Christian spiritual formation conference where one of the keynote speakers confronted so-called consumer Christians who were dependent on consolation from God. The speaker implied that it was immature to want consolation from God. At the end of his talk he asked us to stand up if we were willing to deny ourselves and totally surrender to the Lord. I wanted to stand but couldn't. I feared I would be surrendering to suffering and shame. Later, I realized this experience triggered my implicit trauma memory of being a newborn baby, not able to hold down food or be comforted, and then being alone in a hospital for surgery. *I felt shamed and abandoned for having needs and wanting comfort.* I also felt judged as a childish Christian.

I fell into a Dark Night of spiritual depression. I had taught on God's love, but now I wasn't confident it was true for me. I was wrestling with why God allowed so much suffering. The emotional distress that surfaced was discouraging because I had been in therapy and felt I'd already worked that through. I wasn't able to appreciate the Spirit of Jesus exposing deeper layers of my soul for healing. It didn't feel like grace. I wish I had known about the journey of the CHRIST stages back then, because that would've given me hope and encouraged me to trust that God was doing a good work in me.

In my desperation I reached out to Jane Willard, Dallas' wife, who was a therapist who understood spiritual formation. She didn't want me to drive five hours to get to her. I prayed and sensed the Lord saying, "Kristi, if Mary could travel by donkey for eighty miles to meet with Elizabeth, then you can travel by car that far to meet with Jane!"

Characteristics of the I Stage

The Inner Journey is an opportunity for increasing intimacy with Jesus and his Father, but it often doesn't feel this way at first. In the Psalm 23 journey we're coming out of the dark valley—a time of suffering, faith crisis, or spiritual dryness at The Wall. Then David's prayer leads us to seek comfort in the Shepherd's rod and staff (v. 4). With his rod a shepherd separates headbutting sheep and calls wandering sheep back to the safety of the fold. With his staff he pulls sheep out of pricker bushes or muddy gullies and examines them at night to clean their wool and treat any injuries. Our Shepherd brings us peace in trials and with enemies. With David we sing to the Lord, "You become my delicious feast" (v. 5 TPT).

The soul pivot of the I Stage is a time of digging through distress and questions from The Wall. It can begin as early as young adulthood, but for many people it's not until their midthirties or forties (if ever). Teresa of Jesus says to reach the "higher mansions" of the Second Half we need to live for a long time in the lower ones.[1] At The Wall we question authority and doubt what we've been taught, which may compel us to leave home literally or symbolically. Hopefully this prompts the I Stage in which we work through the limitations of our earlier experiences with family and church, try on new spiritual values, and express a more authentic spirituality. This will help us in life, but initially these changes may evoke feelings of loss, dislocation, disorientation, anxiety, frustration, guilt, emptiness, and aloneness.[2] We need to resist the temptations to shut down our inner distress, distance ourselves from God, stop attending church, keep friends at arm's length, escape into addiction, or revert back to the busyness of the R Stage.

Often we're in a spiritual desert for years till we finally hear the word, "Dry bones, live again!" (see Ezek. 37:5). By being emotionally honest with God and trustworthy people in the I Stage we receive more of the Holy Spirit's inner healing and re-forming. We replace the false self that came unraveled at The Wall with a new self that is increasingly authentic, energetic, free, and engaged in intimate relationships. We learn to find joy and confidence not just in visible blessings but more so in the *spiritual realities* of Christ's cross and kingdom. When we experience Jesus redeeming our pain and failures, we realize that what Satan meant for evil God meant for good (Gen. 50:20; Rom. 8:28).

The emotional turbulence and deep desires of the I Stage can inspire art, music, creative writing, and innovations. It's a rebirth of the C Stage's confidence in Christ—we're rediscovering our first love (Rev. 2:4). We're learning *inside-out spirituality*. We're letting go of the fixed judgments of First Half spirituality in favor of the open-mindedness of Second Half spirituality. Ultimately, the I Stage can facilitate a renewal of the R Stage's productivity at the

S Stage when we tap into the Spirit's energy to create abundant fruitfulness.

People we talk to report a variety of experiences in the Inner Journey:

- "I have been so busy caring for my family and serving the Lord, I didn't realize it was costing me my soul."
- "I'm on a spiritual search because the faith I was taught doesn't work anymore."
- "I feel like a fraud. I teach the Bible to people but I'm questioning my own faith and doubting God."
- "I've already worked so hard to be a healthy person. Yet, I've uncovered more pain from my past to deal with."
- "I long to feel closer to God."
- "I'm appreciating empathy for the first time and it's like coming alive emotionally! My relationships are way better."
- "I'm enjoying new spiritual practices that are refreshing my soul."
- "This inner journey has opened up a whole new intimacy with Jesus for me!"

Path Finder for the I Stage

For each statement below, circle T if it's true of your current experience with God.

YOUR CURRENT EXPERIENCE WITH GOD	TRUE?
1. I long for deeper intimacy with Jesus and the Father.	T
2. I often confess my struggles and shortcomings to God and a friend.	T
3. More than before, I'm processing emotions and issues from my childhood.	T
4. Recently I've been individuating from past spiritual teachers.	T
5. I'm developing a new appreciation of God's love for me.	T

YOUR CURRENT EXPERIENCE WITH GOD	TRUE?
6. I used to feel pressure to measure up, but now I seek God's presence.	T
7. I have an increasing desire to know and follow the Lord.	T
8. If I pray quietly it helps me to sense God's presence (or to desire this).	T

If you circled "true" more often for the I Stage than the previous CHRIST stages, then this may be your current home stage.

Roadblock: Denial of Emotions

Christian psychologist James Finley, who studied under the great monk Thomas Merton, tells a parable that helps us to accept our feelings as part of our faith:

> Imagine that you have a dream in which you are climbing a high mountain. The valley below is where you grew up, where you experienced pain and made many mistakes. You are trying to transcend and leave this place by reaching the summit, on which you will be sublimely holy and one with God.
>
> As the summit comes into view, the wind rising from the valley brings with it the sound of a child crying out in distress. You realize that there is no [good] choice but to go down the mountain to find and help the hurting child. Turning back, you descend into the valley. Following the child's cries, you arrive at the very home you tried to leave behind.
>
> You gently open the door and look inside. Sitting in the corner on the floor is your own wounded child-self, that part of you that [feels] powerlessness and shame. You sit down next to the child on the floor. For a long time you say nothing. Then a most amazing thing happens. As you are putting your arms around this child, you suddenly realize you are on the lofty summit of union with God![3]

Finley's parable illustrates that in order to progress in the journey of our soul we need to feel the longings and hurts of our inner child. If we deny the invitation of the I Stage it thwarts our growth in Christ. Spiritual health emphasizes relationship with

God, repenting of sin, receiving grace, and loving others. Emotional health emphasizes self-awareness, healing hurts, resolving conflicts, and empathy.

Both our spiritual and emotional natures need to be based on *knowing reality* (material and unseen). Spiritual growth without emotional growth leads to illusion and pride. At the same time, emotional growth without spiritual growth is empty and vain. If we focus only on spiritual growth or only on emotional growth, we'll get stuck at The Wall. But integrating the two by following the CHRIST stages helps us to keep growing (see the figure below).

Here are some examples of faith and feelings working together in the I Stage:

- Accepting desolation as a learning opportunity
- Using the Enneagram for awareness of God and self
- Praying Scripture to understand our emotions and inner child
- Giving and receiving empathy to facilitate intimacy with God
- Confessing our sins and family-of-origin wounds to God and a safe friend

Growth in Christ

For me (Kristi), my spiritual growth track got frozen when I felt shamed at the conference for not "surrendering all." Refocusing on my emotional growth through healing prayer ministry and empathy from friends warmed up my soul and got me growing again. For Bill, after his altar experience, he'd been growing emotionally through being in therapy but had been languishing spiritually for a number of years till participating in Ray Ortlund Sr.'s discipleship group inspired his renewal. God made Bill's altar of sacrifice into a table of blessing.

Mirroring Jesus' Emotions

There's an important spiritual psychology that's part of coming alive emotionally and spiritually with Jesus in the Father's world. This is illustrated by my (Bill's) recent day with our grandchild Juliet, who is eighteen months old. She kept exclaiming, "Papa! Papa!" because she enjoys quality attention from me. She gets animated when she sees me looking at her, smiling, and being emotionally present to her. She says "Tic-toc!" and I say "Tic-toc!" and carry her to our grandfather clock. She says "Doodle!" and I say "Doodle!" and sit her in my lap and read her favorite story about a rooster. She says "'Side!" and I say "'Side!" and take hold of her hand as we waddle outside to play. She's discovered the power of words to connect with Papa and fill her love tank!

At the I Stage you especially need soft eyes, mirrored feelings, and warm words to light up your brain cells and your whole being with Christ's embracing presence. Typically, the intensity of your distress at The Wall evokes repressed hurts and unmet needs from earlier in your life, and this can spur you to grow deeper in your salvation.[4] For instance, when you experience a death you feel sad about that loss, plus you experience sadness from previous losses (grief triggers grief). This can move you to seek comfort from a friend and the Lord, which rewires your emotional brain and furthers your soul healing and re-formation in Christ.[5] That's a faith that's heart-deep, embodied, and social.

In our house we have a large mirror with the figure of Jesus etched into the glass. A friend made this for me years ago after she went through my training in lay counseling. When you stand in front of the mirror *you see Jesus' smile in your own face.* In the twelfth century, Clare of Assisi, the soul friend of St. Francis, wrote poetically about spiritual mirroring:

> Cling to Jesus Christ with all your heart! . . .
> His love is what inflames our love . . .
> His graciousness is our joy . . .
> He is your illuminated mirror without blemish—
> Look upon that mirror each day.
> Continually study your face within it . . .
> Contemplate the ineffable charity . . .
> To suffer on the wood of the Cross [for you].[6]

In my Bible study titled "How to Feel Your Emotions with Jesus," I found texts that name *thirty-nine different emotions Jesus felt,* including anxiety, anger, shame, sadness, pain, surprise, curiosity, hope, confidence, love, joy, and peace.[7] For instance, Jesus cried when Lazarus died, got angry at the money changers in the temple, and prayed with great anxiety in the garden of Gethsemane. We're prone to deny the emotions that are distressing, but that banishes them into an unconscious region of our body where they can become toxic and cause sickness, depression, anxiety, addiction, cynicism, isolation, or destructive conflicts with people (e.g., Ps. 32:3–4). Furthermore, trying not to feel an unpleasant emotion can numb our ability to feel any emotion, including the pleasant ones. Instead, you can look into the mirror of Jesus of Nazareth, "the heavenly man" (1 Cor. 15:48). Share your heart with him. See him empathizing with your feelings and thoughts (which are connected) so you can take on the mind of Christ (cf. 1 Cor. 2:16; Heb. 4:15).

When we admire and bond with Jesus the feeler, we naturally put more value on the emotions that we and other people have.[8]

We can do this through meditating on the Gospels and participating in love-one-another relationships in the body of Christ. Connecting with the emotions of Christ helps us to feel and convey his presence in our conversing, praying, playing, preaching, teaching, and working. It helps us to clothe ourselves with Christ's virtues of compassion, kindness, humility, gentleness, and patience (Col. 3:12). Compassion is first in this list of Christ qualities because the others flow from it, and it's perhaps Jesus' most defining characteristic. The word for compassion in Hebrew is *racham*, which means "womb." The implication is that God's motherly care gives us life and holds us in love. Social psychology research backs the importance of caring for feelings by showing that emotional intelligence is the key to success in relationships and work, and it starts with self-awareness.[9]

If you're a thinker or a doer, then paying attention to your emotions may be more difficult for you. This was the case for an investment professional and church leader named Scotty who attended our Institute. "Feelings were not part of my home growing up," he shared. "Everybody kept them inside, but sometimes my dad or someone else would erupt. To me emotions were destructive. My faith was all about reading the Bible, studying it, thinking about it, and trying to do it."

When Scotty was a boy, his dad was an elder and they went to church three times a week. It didn't matter if his friends were playing ball—he had to sit in the hard pews. He was sick and tired of that script. "I'm done giving all the right Christian answers in my small groups. The Bible has become just words on a page to me."

When Scotty saw Jesus' emotions, they mirrored his own emotions he'd been denying. "It brought me a totally new paradigm," he explained. "I studied Jesus' emotions and praised God! It endorsed me having these emotions. I can't tell you how liberating it is to know that anxiety is not a sin and emotions are natural, healthy, even a source of wisdom!" Scotty started meeting with a spiritual director who offered him the hospitality of attentive listening and guided him in learning to draw inspiration from the Psalms to pray his emotions. He beamed. "Now I'm able to talk to my wife and our two high schoolers about how they feel. She's been asking for this for years, but I didn't understand. Now I realize this personal connection is what we both yearn for."

Everyone longs for empathy, whether they admit it or not, and it's crucial to progressing in the I Stage. The Lord's name *Immanuel* means God is with you and cares deeply for you. Empathy is not just for therapy—it's for your family, church, small group, and workplace. Learning to feel your emotions softens your heart for the grace of a deeper experience of Jesus' friendship, the Father's love, and the Spirit's presence and power. To grow in this grace you need to absorb compassionate listening. That's because as a child (or emotional beginner) you learn to feel your own emotions only after a parent (or friend) feels them with you and verbalizes them for you.

Grace: Deeper Experiences of God's Love

In seventeenth-century England, John Wesley's overzealous religion, overworking as a pastor, and lack of care for his emotional needs put him at The Wall for years and left him believing he wasn't truly a Christian. He desperately wanted to experience the love of Jesus that he saw in the Moravian Christians he met on a ship traveling to America. When the ship was tossed about at sea in a terrible storm, Wesley became sick with fear and anxiety—but they were at peace and cheerfully singing hymns to God! He cared for the poor dutifully and somberly—but they did so with ease, lightness, and generosity. He felt empty—but they were alive with God's presence and joy.

Then one day, when Wesley was thirty-four years old, he went to a church meeting where someone read from Martin Luther's writings on grace. Wesley later exclaimed, "I felt my heart strangely warmed!" God used this spark to renew his soul and ultimately to launch the worldwide Methodist revival.[10]

Like Wesley, there have been countless men and women throughout history who were dutiful Christians for many years in the R Stage and then had a deeper experience of God's Spirit in the I Stage. They personally received our Big Brother's incredible offer, "It is time for the realm of God's kingdom to be experienced in its fullness!" (Mark 1:15 TPT). "I have called you friends" (John 15:15). Depending on their tradition, they've described their renewal as "walking in the Spirit," "the life of faith," "death to the self-life," "being filled with the Spirit," "the baptism of the Holy Spirit," "entire sanctification," "whole-hearted consecration," "overcoming power," or "pure love."[11] What great joy it brings when the Spirit's spring of fresh living water gushes up from your belly (see John 7:37–38 KJV).

In the early church it was common for Jesus' disciples to have soul-filling experiences of grace. After Jesus rose from the dead, he breathed the Holy Spirit into his disciples, infusing them with divine peace and forgiveness (John 20:21–23). Paul picks up this teaching, praying fervently in Jesus' name that in our depths we will be filled with love and power from the Spirit of our Father and that we will *keep being filled* (Eph. 3:14–19; 5:18). In Acts we read story after story of people being *flooded* with the life-giving Spirit through practices like waiting on God (1:4; 2:1), devoting their life to God (2:38, 42–43), crying out in prayer (4:31), the laying on of hands (8:17), and preaching the word (10:44). In Acts these immersions in the Spirit are manifested in various ways such as physical heat (2:3; 9:3), joy (13:52; 16:33–34), praying in a heavenly language (2:4; 10:46; 19:6), boldness to witness for Christ (4:31; 19:8; 28:31), or supernatural gifts like words of knowledge and healing (3:1–10; 6:8; 9:17–18; 19:11–12).[12]

C. S. Lewis writes about the need to personally experience the Holy Spirit:

> The union between the Father and the Son is such a live concrete thing that this union itself is also a Person. . . .

The whole dance, or drama, or pattern of this three-Personal life is to be played out in each one of us. . . . There is no other way to the happiness for which we were made. Good things as well as bad, you know, are caught by a kind of infection. If you want to get warm you must stand near the fire: if you want to be wet you must get into the water. If you want joy, power, peace, eternal life, you must get close to, or even into, the thing that has them. . . . They are a great fountain of energy and beauty spurting up at the very centre of reality. . . .

Now the whole offer which Christianity makes is this: that we can, if we let God have His way, come to share in the life of Christ. . . . We shall love the Father as He does and the Holy Ghost will arise in us.[13]

"We all have been called to the depths of Christ," writes the seventeenth-century French spiritual mother Jean Guyon. She describes a "deep, inward relationship to Jesus Christ" that is simply "the turning and yielding of your heart to the Lord . . . the expression of love within your heart for Him." She adds, "You may think yourself the one farthest from a deep experience with the Lord [but] in fact, the Lord has especially chosen you! You are the one most suited to know Him well."[14]

To know the Lord deeply is to discover that the eternal Creator, the God who calls the stars by name, the Ruler of the universe, the sovereign Lawgiver, and the holy Judge of all is your dear Papa![15] You can approach the throne of God and climb up to sit in your Daddy-King's lap. This is who God wants to be to you, so the Spirit of grace keeps reminding you that *Jesus' Abba is your Abba too* (Rom. 8:15; Gal. 4:6). Brennan Manning discovered this and testified, "The greatest gift I have ever received from Jesus Christ is the Abba experience. . . . My dignity as Abba's child is my most coherent sense of self."[16]

The fatherly love of God for you is not just a theological principle—it can be your operating reality. Even in a world with terrorists and infectious diseases we can find security and strength from dwelling in the spiritual reality of the Father's world. *Do you know that Abba God is very fond of you? Treats you tenderly? Really likes you?!*

Inner Healing

As I (Kristi) shared earlier, I struggled to trust God's love when I was younger. When I met with Jane Willard for emotional healing prayer ministry she asked about my developmental history and traced the roots of my depression to self-hatred, which went all the way back to that scene of feeling abandoned as an infant in the hospital. My mom loved me very much and found the doctor who gave me a life-saving surgery, but in those days a mother wasn't allowed to stay with her baby in the hospital, so I was often left alone, crying in a cold, sterile room with no one to hold me. That early trauma, along with being a feeler in a family of thinkers, left me judging and hating myself as "too sensitive and emotional."

In my first healing prayer session with Jane, the Holy Spirit evoked my implicit traumatic memory of my surgery. It had been repressed in my body and subconscious, but now through quiet prayer, the Spirit showed me my infant self, isolated and shivering in a room with bright lights shining on me. I was crying and screaming in terror and couldn't be held or comforted. This was an experience of abandonment depression like we discussed in the last chapter.

Then Jane asked me, "Can you see Jesus? Where is he? Ask him to help you see what he wants to do for you." We were silent together for a few minutes as I kept my mind open to the Spirit. Suddenly, in my mind I saw Jesus come to hold me. Instead of being blinded by the hospital lights, I felt *delighted in* by him as he looked into my eyes and comforted me!

I told Jane what I saw and she asked me who else was in the room with my infant self. I saw my mother, grandparents, and an aunt who I was close to as a little girl. Then I saw Bill (which must be because as an adult, he's cared for my emotions). Then Jane offered, "I'd like you to see me there too. I'm really happy that you were born too. I want to be there for you."

I started to cry—I was so touched in my heart. I felt safe, warm, and held. I felt healing beginning deep inside me. I felt gratitude and joy. I felt God's presence filling me with pure love! We've been using the spiritual term *consolation* to describe this kind of a felt blessing. Let's use a different term here: therapists like us call this a *corrective emotional experience*. When you share your emotions with a support person, internalize compassion, and deeply bond, it reformats the hard drive of your soul in divine health.

After we were done praying, Jane cautioned me, "There are some really young places in you that God is touching and healing. You need to be very intentional to protect this tender growth and not get too busy in ministry. Save time and space for your soul to keep receiving God's love." It felt selfish to me—like I shouldn't need that—but Jane insisted, "It'll be death to your little girl if you let yourself get preoccupied with ministry in this season."

I had been in the Responsibilities in Ministry stage—very busy with our kids, my work as a therapist, and a few ministries in our church—but now I needed to cut back on my outward activity to clear space and energy to go deeper in this new inward season of restoration. I continued the healing prayer sessions and also was helped by heart-engaging practices like praying Scripture and soul friendship. Slowly but surely, I began enjoying the nearness of my Father in the I Stage, which I'd been missing at The Wall. As Henri Nouwen says, I heard "the voice that calls me the Beloved" and felt increasing desire to "hear that voice longer and more deeply. It is like discovering a well in the desert. Once you have touched wet ground, you want to dig deeper."[7]

It was similar for Madeline, a pastor we worked with in our Institute. She had just gotten through The Wall and was learning to give and receive empathy as she processed her ministry stress and deficits from her childhood. She was also engaging in spiritual formation practices and feeling a rising longing for intimacy with Jesus that she wanted to share with her church. She told us, "As a pastor I want to bring what I'm learning to the people I shepherd." But she wisely discerned, "The Spirit has not released me. This is a season of *loving destruction*: the Lord has been taking apart my productive self and calling me to rest in his arms." She needed to protect and deepen the work of the Spirit in her heart. Later, she would need gentle wisdom for how to share what she'd been learning with people in her church, most of whom were in earlier CHRIST stages.

Take Heart

I (Bill) will never forget the time I was having lunch with Ray Ortlund Sr. and he looked at me with a bright face and urged, "Bill, be ull und only for Juuuu!" Another time Ray encouraged me, "I love your heart for Jesus! We need psychologists who express affection and devotion for our Lord. Don't be shy. Be with other people the way you are with me—let your heart for Jesus hang out." That's why I'm sharing vulnerably with you now.

In these soul talks it was like the sun breaking through the clouds. The Spirit of Joy surged into my being as I realized I could be enthusiastically devoted to Jesus like Ray! After this, Kristi and I went on a two-day private retreat with Ray and his wife, Anne. When they laid their hands on us and prayed over us at the end, I was bold to pray for a double anointing of the Holy Spirit that operated in Ray, like Elisha did with Elijah (2 Kings 2:9). Immediately and continuing for two weeks, I felt a tingling warmth on the back of my neck and shoulders. Sometimes this sensation returns, like even now as I'm sharing this story with you!

I believe this to be a manifestation of the Spirit of Jesus' presence and power, like "the Jesus burn" that the Emmaus disciples experienced (Luke 24:32).[18] To use C. S. Lewis' analogy, I caught the virus of devotion to Jesus from Ray.[19] Lewis described such an encounter as a paradox of experiencing "stabs of joy."[20] Teresa of Jesus called it a "delectable-wound" of being love-sick.[21] It's a happy-sad encounter of touching into the wonder of being lavishly loved by the Lord and yet knowing there is so much more love that's just out of reach. There's a joyous hope of more heavenly warmth to come and yet a painful regret of all the times that your heart devotion for God has been lacking.

Both the happy and the sad sides of God's love leave you yearning for more. Yet, even though the feeling of the Spirit's consolation comes and goes, *you are not left feeling empty*—as with the fleeting pleasures of worldly entertainments or addictions. Rather, you feel a sense of fulfillment and dignity.

In the I Stage it's like the wind of the Spirit changes direction to move you through The Wall with empathy and into the warm love of Jesus and his Papa. But this is not like being a passive leaf blowing in a breeze—it's like being an eagle that perches on a treetop, waits for an updraft of wind, and then opens its wings to soar into the heavens (see Isa. 40:31). My part for growing in intimacy with God was to "take heart" for Jesus from Ray.[22] Nathaniel did this when he followed Philip to Jesus and traded his fig-tree world for Jesus' world in which angels ascended and descended between earth and heaven as with Jacob's ladder (see John 1:43–51; cf. Gen. 28:10–19). Similarly, the Canaanite woman took heart from Jesus' smile, and like an indefatigable puppy dog she overcame the disciples' prejudice against her and prevailed upon the Master to heal her daughter (see Matt. 15:21–28 TPT).

While Kristi and I were writing this chapter, I woke up one morning with a smile on my face because in my dream I'd been holding hands with *Jesu* and singing the great hymn, "He walks with me and talks with me and tells me I am His own."[23] The night before I'd been meditating on the lyrics of Bach's anthem "Jesu, Joy of Man's Desiring."

But often we don't feel desire for God. What do we do then? Are we just to soldier on with serving God and doing what's right? That's the mentality that's typical after a number of years in

Responsibilities in Ministry, and it can lead to a fade-out, burnout, or blowout. Instead, when we find that we're not longing for God, we can learn to *long* to long for God. We can nurture affectionate reverence for Jesu and Abba through heart-awakening disciplines. We don't do these exercises to prove our love for God but to make space to hear the voice of God call us the Beloved (which is Henri Nouwen's definition of a spiritual discipline).[24] This helps us to progress in the Inner Journey and the Second Half of our pilgrimage.

Which of these hungry-heart disciplines might help you to take heart for Jesus and enjoy your life anew with him in Abba's world?

- Repeat the breath prayer "Abba, I belong to you." Feel Jesus' passion for his Father catch fire in your heart.[25]
- Imagine yourself in a Gospel passage with Jesus.[26]
- Engage in soul talk with a spiritual friend who is intelligently smitten with Jesus Christ.
- Sing a verse from the Psalms like, "Lord, earth has nothing I desire besides you!" (73:25).
- Fast from food as you feast on God's word (Matt. 4:4).[27]
- Use silent prayers to stream the Spirit's love from your heart to someone else.
- Read a classic of devotion to Christ (see the excerpt in the soul care practice below).[28]

Trail Markers for the I Stage

AGE	18+ (usually 30+, if ever)
FAITH	Authenticity and acceptance
COGNITIVE DEVELOPMENT	Self-reflection and intrinsic beliefs
ROADBLOCK & TEMPTATIONS	Denying emotions, needs, or problems Distrusting "spiritual formation" Avoiding intimacy with people or God Self-absorption or overwhelmed by emotions Judging your needs, emotions, or faults Not relying on the Bible as inspired by the Spirit
IMAGES OF GOD	Jesus as Friend, God as Abba, and Holy Spirit
GRACE	Deeper experiences of God's love
LESSONS	Moving from rules to relationship with Jesus and Abba Confessing sin and distress to God and friends Repairing emotional-relational problems from past Leaving home and authorities to express own faith Renewing image of God as loving during suffering Wholehearted submission/devotion to the Lord
SPIRITUAL DISCIPLINES	Praying the Psalms Soul friendships (with empathy) Enneagram or other self-assessments Lectio Divina (Scripture meditation) Quiet prayer with Bible verse or image Reading devotional classics Healing prayer Fasting while feasting on God's Word Praising the Lord with adoration Sabbath Journaling your dreams
CHURCH MINISTRIES	Recovery sponsors Healing prayer intercessors Lay counseling Discipleship training Spiritual formation teaching and writing Spiritual leadership (e.g., elder board)

············ **Guidebook Scriptures for the I Stage** ············

- **Intimacy with Jesus is the best life:** "Nothing is as wonderful as knowing Christ Jesus my Lord. I have given up everything else and count it all as garbage. All I want is Christ" (Phil. 3:8 CEV).

- **The Father loves you unconditionally:** "Look with wonder at the depth of the Father's marvelous love that he has lavished on us! He has called us and made us his very own *beloved* children" (1 John 3:1 TPT).

- **Emotionally vulnerable prayers are helpful:** "Search me, God, and know my heart; test me and know my anxious thoughts. See if there is any offensive way in me, and lead me in the way everlasting" (Ps. 139:23–24).

- **God heals past sins and pains:** "The People of Israel gathered for a fast . . . and confessed their sins and the iniquities of their parents. . . . They read from the Book of The Revelation of God" (Neh. 9:2–3 MSG).

- **With Jesus feast on God's words of life:** "Jesus answered by quoting Deuteronomy: 'It takes more than bread to stay alive. It takes a steady stream of words from God's mouth'" (Matt. 4:4 MSG).

- **Take heart for Jesus with a soul friend:** The disciples on the Emmaus road "began telling each other how their hearts had felt strangely warm as he talked with them and explained the Scriptures during the walk down the road" (Luke 24:32 TLB).

- **Breathe in the Spirit of Jesus:** "Then [Jesus] took a deep breath and breathed into them. 'Receive the Holy Spirit,' he said. 'If you forgive someone's sins, they're gone for good'" (John 20:22–23 MSG).

Soul Care Practice

Enthrallment with Jesus

Enthralling our minds with God is the *primary* objective in Dallas Willard's "Curriculum for Christlikeness."[29] It's soul fuel for growing in grace, especially at the I Stage. Yet, the joy and power of stirring up affectionate reverence for the Lord is often missing in Christian education and service. Frank Laubach, one of my (Bill's) author mentors, has supported my faith in this way. A few years ago, I got hold of an original, signed copy of his seventy-year-old book on prayer. His words came with the Breath of Life and riveted my heart to Jesus Christ. I'd like to share an excerpt to help you join the ministry of the Holy Spirit who continually moves on your heart to be captivated with Jesu and his Abba (Rom. 8:15; 1 Cor. 12:3).

> The knowledge that can save the world is already ours. It is the way of Jesus Christ, what He is, what He teaches, and how He transforms people. When we join our thoughts to Him we are in an immense river pressing through every race and every nation. Jesus has already proved to be the world's greatest blessing. He has not

yet been able to save it from its present state, because not enough of us are thinking and acting upon His ideals. . . .

Christ is not only the most powerful person the world has ever known; He is the *noblest*. All the highest ideals since His day . . . have sprung from His teachings. . . . The greatest way to help Christ conquer the world is . . . by thinking about Him and His Kingdom *as much as we can*. . . . If we keep Him in our thoughts persistently . . . we shall radio thoughts of Christ to the minds of [people around us].

How can we saturate our minds with Christ? There is but one way . . . to read His life in the four Gospels so often that we know it by heart. . . . We need determined wills to protect [our study] with Christ from competing interests. Busy people are under constant temptation to allow Bible reading to be crowded out . . . until omission becomes a habit. Then they find the edge of their interest dulling and their attention wavering. The *only* protection we have is to consider the hour of devotions a sacred engagement with God, and to decline all interrupting invitations.[30]

The first time I read these words I sensed the Spirit say, "Bill, the gospel of Jesus is the greatest story ever told! Get caught up in it as the drama of your life!" At that point I'd read all four Gospels many times, but never a whole Gospel in one sitting like Laubach. I realized that often I was excited to watch a two-hour movie or sports event, so why not approach the Gospels that way?

I spent the next two hours on my knees in my prayer room reading the Gospel of John straight through. When I finished, I started skipping and jumping around our house and exclaiming, "Christ is risen! Christ is risen!" I was singing and waving my arms in jubilation. The Good News got deep into me, and I needed to express it. I came more alive in the Kingdom of the Heavens. Since then I have listened to, read, or watched an entire Gospel without interruption over one hundred times.[31] More than ever, Christ's life, love, and leadership are shaping my life and ministry.

Taking Heart from Paul

Paul, the apostle of grace, is a great example of a person whose life was filled and overflowing with the presence of God (as we saw in his story at the end of chapter 2). A primary reason for this is because he had a discipline of enthralling his mind and heart with God through Jesus Christ. He spent three years in solitude in the desert meditating on his encounter with the risen Christ, what the Damascus disciples told him about Jesus, and what the Old Testament prophesied about the Messiah (Gal. 1:17). He absorbed Peter's story, which became the Gospel of Mark (Gal. 1:18). Then Paul probably worked with Luke in gathering the eyewitness stories of Jesus that make up the third Gospel.[32] Paul's saturation in the gospel of Christ is displayed in his letters, which continually adore Jesus and glean from his life, grace, wisdom, cross, and resurrection.

For instance, Paul's letter to the Colossians gives the gospel in miniature. His message is that in every domain of knowledge, work, relationship, and life, and in every square inch of the earth and the entire universe, Jesus Christ is supreme. It takes thirteen minutes to read Paul's letter out loud, and he speaks of Christ more than once every *ten seconds*. I want my blogs, books, podcasts, seminars, and sermons to be that saturated with the sweet name and spirit of Jesus! Here are some highlights from Colossians for captivating our intelligence and affections with the Lord Jesus:

> We look at this Son and see the God who cannot be seen. . . . Everything got started in him and finds its purpose in him. He was there before any of it came into existence and holds it all together up to this moment. . . .
>
> He is supreme. . . . From beginning to end he's there, towering far above everything, everyone. . . . Everything of God finds its proper place in him. . . . All the broken and dislocated pieces of the universe—people and things, animals and atoms—get properly

fixed and fit together in vibrant harmonies, all because of his death, his blood poured down from the cross. . . .

Christ brought you over to God's side and put your lives together, whole and holy in his presence. You don't walk away from a gift like that! You stay grounded and steady in that bond of trust, constantly tuned in to the Message, careful not to be distracted or diverted. . . . Christ is in you, so therefore you can look forward to sharing in God's glory. . . .

All the richest treasures of wisdom and knowledge are embedded in [Christ]. . . . You received Christ Jesus, the Master; now *live* him. You're deeply rooted in him. You're well constructed upon him. . . .

Let every detail in your lives—words, actions, whatever—be done in the name of the Master, Jesus, thanking God the Father every step of the way.[33]

Soul Talk

1. How does it help you to see Bible stories with Jesus experiencing the full range of negative and positive emotions (e.g., anxiety, anger, shame, sadness, pain, surprise, curiosity, hope, confidence, love, joy, peace)?

2. What is your response to spiritual mother Jean Guyon's saying "We have all been called to the depths of Christ"?

3. What memories or feelings surfaced for you when you reflected on Finley's parable of reaching the mountain summit in the Roadblock section of this chapter?

4. What did you feel as you read the Guidebook Scriptures for the I Stage?

5. What was your experience with enthralling your mind and heart with Jesus Christ as Paul did?

Packing List for the S Stage

In Spirit-Led Ministry we learn to live and work in Jesus' easy yoke. To journey into this stage you'll need:

1. Patience to wait on the wind of the Spirit
2. Practices for hearing God's voice
3. Trust in the Lord's sovereignty
4. Holy Spirit's anointing on your ministry

8

The S Stage: Spirit-Led Ministry

Our greatest joy and impact is to act with the presence and power of the Spirit to serve others.

> You anoint my head with oil;
> My cup runs over.
>
> Psalm 23:5 NKJV

In college I (Bill) read some old spiritual books written by monks, which inspired me to take a private retreat at a monastery. I wanted to pray about my sense that God was calling me into ministry as a Christian psychologist. But my experience in the abbey left me spooked by the monks in black hoods. When I met with one of them for spiritual direction, he handed me a religious book full of theological jargon. I walked away shaking my head. The only thing I got from that book was the word "grace," which was in the title. It seemed that God wanted to teach me about grace, but I couldn't find any in the book, so I threw it in the garbage!

For three days of solitude, silence, and fasting I walked aimlessly in the woods on the monastery property. I was hungry, lonely, and tired. I didn't hear God's voice. I didn't sense the Spirit's presence. I didn't learn anything about grace. I didn't want to serve Christ in a counseling ministry anymore. *I didn't even want to be a Christian anymore!*

As I walked around, I had flashbacks from the previous three months and my summer job in a meat market. I kept remembering the butchers persecuting me for being a Christian, spewing out vulgarities, and abusing me verbally and emotionally. It was horrible! In the first week I told God that I wanted to quit, but I heard him say, "No. This is what I have for you this summer. I want to teach you and love you in a new way." So every day on my lunch hour I read 1 Peter, which is about enduring suffering. I clung to God's words, but *they didn't seem true for me:* I didn't feel any "great mercy" or "living hope" (1:3) or see any faith-gold coming from my furnace of affliction (1:6–7), nor did I feel restored and strengthened by "the God of all grace" (5:10).

I kept saying to my mom and a friend, "I thought God loved me. Why would my Father want me to suffer like this? Where is God's grace?" I felt abandoned by God and confused. And I felt like a failure as a Christian for not being a better witness for Christ to my coworkers.

Characteristics of the S Stage

When our Shepherd anoints our head with oil in Psalm 23, it's to heal our wounds. Later, we're surprised to discover that his oil also anoints us for ministry. (Recall that we use the word "ministry" to refer to *any* work that's dedicated to loving God and people.) We give thanks to God with David, saying, "My cup runs over!" (v. 5 NKJV). The Shepherd leads his sheep to streams and springs. When these dry up in the summer, he leads us to wells, and if no wells are near then he offers us a drink from his own large flask of water. As we sit around our Shepherd-King's banquet table, there's always a servant standing nearby ready to refill cups. It's a picture of the soul brimming with the Spirit of grace. At the S Stage we're learning to minister to others out of the overflow of God's love—we're blessed to be a blessing to others (2 Cor. 9:14; Phil. 1:9 NLT).

Recall that at The Wall we took off the mask of our false self, and in the I Stage we continued that unmasking process to express more of our true self. Building on this growing self-awareness and God-awareness, in Spirit-Led Ministry we're learning to live and work from our authentic self, created by God, redeemed by Christ Jesus, and anointed by Holy Spirit. (Notice we dropped "the" before "Holy Spirit" to emphasize that the third member of the Trinity is a *Person* for us to relate to and not just a force.[1]) The S Stage is like catching the wind of the Spirit in your sail. Devoted to the Lord's service and empowered by Holy Spirit, we can have sustaining joy and power, so we're not as prone to burnout as in the R Stage. We're learning to integrate our work and prayer in the Cycle of Grace, so our doing flows out of being with Jesus Christ as we walk and work with him in his easy yoke (Matt. 11:28–30). Increasingly, we have an inner center of deep-rooted calmness and confidence as our beloved *Parakletos* (Holy Spirit)[2] breathes benevolence within us and strengthens us to carry out the divine will to love our friends, neighbors, and even our enemies in Jesus' name.

Except for a few young people who are so-called "old souls," most Christ-followers do not experience Spirit-Led Ministry until their forties or later, if ever. In the S Stage our faith mindset matures to appreciate paradoxes and integrate apparent contradictions, like God's sovereign will and our personal responsibility to make choices.[3] We further our transition from either-or to both-and thinking to become increasingly open to gleaning wisdom from sources that are outside our tradition. Like George Fox, the seventeenth-century founder of the Quakers, we appreciate the Light of Christ lighting on every person.[4] We're in

Erikson's psychosocial stage of Generativity, seeking to leave a legacy by offering our creativity and love to those who are younger.[5] But Satan tries to divert us from relying on the Spirit of Love by enticing us into the pseudospirituality of emotionalism or impulsiveness.[6]

The S Stage also correlates with Teresa of Jesus' sixth spiritual mansion, which emphasizes deepening submission to God's will, mystical experiences, and passion for knowing and serving the Lord.[7] We return to the outward, work-oriented focus of Responsibilities in Ministry, but in a new way: *Now we don't depend on our own abilities or other people, but on Holy Spirit within us and around us.* Holy Spirit, who raised Jesus from the dead, gives vitality to our bodies as we join our life with Christ risen in the heavenly realms of the Kingdom of Light (Rom. 8:11; Eph. 2:6). Even as we serve God, we can enjoy the "fellowship of the Transfigured Face."[8]

Here are some testimonies of people living in the abundance and adventure of the S Stage:

- "I don't have the same ambition as before—I simply want to be part of what Christ is doing."
- "I stopped preaching how-to sermons to focus on discipleship to Christ. People are growing, but our church attendance has declined."
- "I'm in a season of waiting to see what God will do, but I'm surprisingly content."
- "Often I sense the Spirit with me and helping me—even before I consciously pray."
- "Discerning what God seems to be saying and doing is key to my ministry."
- "It's really true. I'm living a resurrection life that's adventurously expectant. My continual prayer is, 'What's next, Papa?' (Rom. 8:15 MSG)."

- "I feel Christ's presence as he uses me to care for people."
- "Learning to walk and work in Jesus' easy yoke has given me new freedom and power!"

Path Finder for the S Stage

For each statement below, circle T if it's true of your current experience with God:

YOUR CURRENT EXPERIENCE WITH GOD	TRUE?
1. I don't worry about the results of ministry—I keep following Jesus' lead.	T
2. I've persevered with faith through a Dark Night of the Soul.	T
3. I've had special words or experiences of God that are hard to explain.	T
4. I sense the Spirit's presence and power in my daily life and work.	T
5. In stress I often can sense God helping me to be unhurried and at peace.	T
6. I enjoy serving in Jesus' easy yoke even if people don't recognize me.	T
7. I share my hurts, struggles, and progress to help others grow.	T
8. I like to be still and quiet because it helps me hear God or sense the Spirit.	T

If you circled "true" more often for the S Stage than the other CHRIST stages, this may be your current home stage.

Roadblock: Dark Night of the Soul

There's a story that one day Teresa of Jesus was walking to a prayer service when she got caught in a fierce rainstorm and fell into the mud. She looked up to the Lord in heaven and quipped, "If that is how you treat your friends, it's no wonder you have so few of them!" To get muddy is a little thing, but to feel rejected or mistreated by God is hugely painful and can derail our journey in the CHRIST stages, sending us back to The Wall. The psalmist and other Bible writers often struggled through dark times of desolation, feeling that God's face was hidden.[9]

Teresa's friend John of the Cross called these spiritual trials the Dark Night of the Soul. He was a barefoot monk who stood just four feet, eleven inches tall and had a huge influence for God. But it came at a high price as he was brutally persecuted and imprisoned by religious authorities for teaching contemplative prayer. They flogged him severely to pressure him to renounce the practice of praying quietly to Jesus in his heart, but he would not stop. They confined him to a tiny dark and dank cell. They fed him rations of bread and water and gave him nothing to read and no pen or paper for writing. He was plagued by a horrible darkness of God's absence. Yet, as he lay crouched in his cramped prison, he composed love poems to Jesus like this one:

> One dark night,
> Fired with love's urgent longings
> —Ah, the sheer grace!—
> I went out unseen,
> My house being now all stilled.[10]

After nine months in solitary confinement, John escaped to Teresa's convent, and there he provided spiritual direction ministry and wrote about the Dark Night of the Soul. He taught that a Dark Night is not because of sin, lack of spiritual discipline, depression, or another problem. Instead, *God is purposefully withdrawing the felt sense of his love to mature us.* John explained that in a season of spiritual dryness God is weaning us off from the bottle of spiritual consolation so we can learn to trust the loving presence of Christ and bless other people, even when we're in difficult circumstances. We think our blackout is because God is far away, but actually we're *blinded by the nearness of God's bright presence shining in our face.*[11]

Feeling deserted and disoriented, it's tempting to turn back to the I Stage, hoping for consolation. Instead, we can learn to trust the mysterious work of the Spirit of Jesus and the Father in the S Stage. In due time we can become "fired with love's urgent longings" for God, which leads to experiencing "sheer grace." With the psalmist we can pray, "Whom have I in heaven but you? And earth has nothing I desire besides you. My flesh and my heart may fail, but God is the strength of my heart and my portion forever" (Ps. 73:25–26). As we keep saying, even in a season of desolation there are hidden blessings to discover.

The little barefoot monk distinguished between two different kinds of soul darkness: the Dark Night of the *Senses* and the Dark Night of the *Spirit* (the table below summarizes their differences). Our senses (emotions) and spirit (will) are two different functions of our soul. When our sense of God's blessings is shut down, we feel deprived or rejected. If our intention (will) to serve the Lord in a particular way is cut off, then we feel unimportant or disrespected. In both instances the Lord is lovingly teaching us that the best blessings are not outward but *inward*—they're "treasures hidden in the darkness" (Isa. 45:3 NLT). In the Dark Night of the Senses we can learn to find delight in knowing Jesus even when we don't feel him in our circumstances. In the Dark Night of the Spirit we can learn to flourish in sharing the love of Jesus with our neighbors even if no one seems to appreciate us.

Teresa referred to Dark Nights as "periods of aridity" that we typically experience later in our pilgrimage to prepare us for the union with Christ that is the goal of our journey.[12] We've found that the first night season tends to occur in the I Stage and the second in the S Stage.

When I was in my early twenties in the meat market and monastery, I experienced a Dark Night of the Senses. I was in the R Stage at The Wall and touching into the I Stage. (Recall that our growth in the stages of faith is not linear—it's a back-and-forth process.) I felt that God was not protecting me from being mistreated and was not caring for me or blessing me. I didn't have this teaching back then, so I didn't comprehend what God was doing. Looking

	DARK NIGHT OF THE SENSES	DARK NIGHT OF THE SPIRIT
Two Dark Nights of the Soul		
CHRIST STAGE	Inner Journey	Spirit-Led Ministry
DEFINITION	Senses (feelings) darkened	Spirit (will) darkened
EMOTIONAL TRIALS	Not feeling blessed by God Feeling abandoned	Not feeling used by God Feeling insignificant
GOAL	Trust God as loving when he's not blessing you how you want	Love God and neighbor when he's not blessing you how you want
SELF-DENIAL DISCIPLINE	Learning to live not just by bread but by God's words (Matt. 4:4)	Learning to live not just by bread but by doing God's will and works of love (John 4:34)
BLESSING	Able to enjoy intimacy with Jesus during trials	Able to serve God and people during trials

back, I see that Holy Spirit was drawing me into a new grace at the I Stage, increasing my awareness of my emotions and my desire for closeness with Christ Jesus and his Abba.

In contrast, when I was in my early thirties and discerned that God was asking me to stop writing Christian books, which I shared about in the opening of chapter 1, I was in a Dark Night of the Spirit and having an early experience with the S Stage. At that time I lost the will to serve God. I was discouraged that the Lord didn't want me to use my gift of writing. I felt like a racehorse stuck at the gate for a number of years. That gate became The Wall, and I lost hope of being a published author again. While my family and personal life were mostly good, it was a dark and dry season in my career and ministry. Eventually I realized that God was wonderfully caring for me by asking for my *heart* and not my gift. I discovered surprising and increasing joy in practicing the downward mobility of simply loving people for Jesus' sake. Then the Lord called me into a new ministry of writing that has been very fruitful.

Shortly after I found new freedom and joy in my relationship with God, Kristi went into a Dark Night of the Spirit, which she described in chapter 7. In her intense season of desolation, her spirit-will was darkened by all the suffering that God allowed her and others to experience. She was scared and unwilling to fully surrender to God. She struggled through this till she learned to take heart for God by joining Mary's prayer of submission, "Let it be to me according to your word" (Luke 1:38 NKJV). She fought to keep offering her tender heart of mercy to hurting people—even when it brought her desolation. After a few years, she emerged into the S Stage's grace of living and serving in the heavenly realms of the Kingdom of God, enjoying the wide-open spaces of beauty, intimacy, and adventure.

Grace: Surprise Blessings to Share

Let's return to my story from the summer before my senior year of college. After I'd spent three days of desolate wandering in the woods of the monastery, my mom picked me up, and since it was Sunday we drove to church. In worship we were singing "Our God Reigns" from Isaiah 52:7: "How beautiful on the mountains are the feet of those who bring good news." Finally, I felt some consolation! I got caught up in the immersive experience of praising the Lord with the congregation. Then, out of the blue, I had an extraordinary vision. Without trying to imagine or think anything, I saw myself before a great mountain, like the one Moses climbed to get the Ten Commandments. I wanted to ascend into God's presence, but I felt totally incapable and ashamed, as I had among the butchers and the monks.

Then Jesus appeared in the scene. He was shining radiantly and walking down the mountain to me. It was kind of like a dream in that as he circled down the mountain, we never lost eye contact, even when the mountain was between us. He looked at me the way I imagined he'd looked at Peter after his denials (Luke 22:61). *There's fiery love in his eyes. He's looking right into my soul. He knows all my sins, all my thoughts and feelings, all my longings, all the good in me and all the bad in me. Yet he loves me unconditionally and totally!* I was flooded with Jesus' compassion and mercy.

When Jesus got to the bottom of the mountain, he came right to me. He picked me up, put me over his shoulder like a sack of potatoes, and carried me up the mountain of God. As he carried me, a mob gathered who insulted him, spit on him, yelled at him, and thrashed him with sticks. But nothing was hurting me—he took all the pain. Meanwhile, in church we were still singing about the feet of Jesus bringing us good news. Set across Jesus' shoulders, all I could see were his feet that were bringing *me* good news! Then I realized that *I* was the cross on Jesus' back. He suffered and died for me, for the forgiveness of my sins. He carried me up the mountain and into new intimacy with God.

Jesus does the same for you. He carries you into God's loving presence. Pause a moment to breathe, imagine this scene, and smile your thanks to Jesus . . . It's true for you too!

George Fox calls this an "opening" from heaven.[13] In my case I was released from the guilt and shame I'd been feeling after the meat market persecutions, and the Spirit of Jesus brought me grace. *Grace.* That was the word the Lord had given me in the title of that boring religious book. I'd preached on grace, but *now I had a fresh experience of God's grace.* Looking back, I can see this heavenly touch of union with Christ drew me to go deeper into the Inner Journey through counseling, psychology classes, and soul friendships. Then I got my first tastes of Spirit-Led Ministry as I learned how to rely on the Spirit's love and power (the Cycle of Grace) as I taught and counseled other students.

My story illustrates how Dark Night desolations and mystical consolations tend to go together, though they may be separated by long periods of time. We often see this in the Bible. Job's sufferings, Hannah's infertility (1 Sam. 1:1–28), and Paul's thorn in the flesh (2 Cor. 12:1–10) were all connected with special blessings from God that brought them exuberant joy.

The Three Lights

After my months of spiritual dryness in a Dark Night, the wonderful vision the Spirit gave me came out of the blue. But my prior discernment that God was calling me to persevere in my meat-market trial came through intentional listening and waiting. What can you do to hear God when you're needing to make a decision or cope with a difficult situation? F. B. Meyer, the great nineteenth-century English pastor, described three lights that help us discern the Lord's voice and purposes:

> God's impressions within and His Word without are always corroborated by His providence around, and we should quietly wait until these three focus into one point. . . .
>
> If you do not know what you ought to do, stand still until you do. And when the time comes for action, circumstances, like glow-worms, will sparkle along your path. You will become so sure that you are right, when God's three witnesses concur, that you could not be surer though an angel beckoned you on.[14]

In our Soul Shepherding Institute, we unpack the three lights of spiritual discernment as a GPS navigator:

GPS for Hearing God

GOD'S WORD

SPIRIT-IMPRESSIONS   PROVIDENCE

Notice that spiritual messages and consolations have their source in God's Word, but we experience them in our circumstances and with the subjective faculties of our thoughts and feelings. Yet, these heavenly touches transcend our senses and are a matter of faith in God's providence directing us.

Ignatius' wisdom for discerning the Lord's voice can help you read your GPS. To make a sound decision he suggests you make yourself like a neutral pointer in the middle of a balance or a passive weather vane that points in whichever direction the wind blows.[15] You're seeking to become indifferent, relaxed about any course of action. This probably requires talking through the options and any anxious feelings with the Lord and a friend who is a good listener. Receiving empathy helps you to experience catharsis, which fosters the calm heart and clear mind that facilitate discernment of God's best.[16] Like the weather vane that's ready for the wind to move it, you're waiting for the "good Spirit"[17] to move your thoughts and emotions in the best direction. Dallas Willard described this to me as "abandoning outcomes to God."[18]

Hearing God's Voice

One night when we were in college, as Bill and I (Kristi) were eating basketfuls of tortilla chips at a restaurant, he shared his vision of Jesus on the mountain. I was drawn to his spiritual experience, but it challenged me. I'd heard preachers and friends talk about hearing God speak. They sounded so confident and assured, and I felt like I was missing out. I judged myself: *I must be a phony because I don't hear God's voice like they do.* I felt confused when they would boldly proclaim, "The Lord says . . ." but it didn't sound like something the Lord would say. For instance, a friend was sure he'd heard God's voice telling him to start a business, but it led him to overwork and it became a devastating financial loss. He thought he was trusting God, but it seemed he was following his own dream.

Maybe you've known people who believed God led them to marry someone, move, or make a risky investment, only to admit after the fact that they were wrong. How do you know if a word, vision, or other mystical experience is from God? What if it's just your own projection? What if it's Satan masquerading as an angel of light (2 Cor. 11:14)? What if it's all the pizza you ate?! How do you distinguish between these different spirits (1 Cor. 12:7, 10)? These difficulties lead many people to decide they can't hear God's voice or that the only true words the Lord speaks are in the Bible.

But Jesus taught that it's as natural for his apprentices to hear God's voice as it is for sheep to hear their shepherd's voice (John 10:3–5). I see this every day in how my cat Charlie responds to my voice. Throughout the Bible we see many examples of people receiving spiritual messages or visits from God, and we may have similar experiences.[19]

There are a number of striking characteristics to the words, visions, or touches from Holy Spirit that help us discern that they are truly from the Lord. When God speaks to us it's normally a still, small voice or gentle whisper like Elijah heard in the cave (1 Kings 19:12). John of the Cross poetically calls this "the whistling of love-stirring breezes."[20] But on the practical level we're simply receiving into our mind thoughts, feelings, or images from God, as was the case for Peter on the rooftop (Acts 10:9–21). The content of these messages will always be consistent with the Bible.

Perhaps the most defining characteristic of a divine message is the tone of God's voice. It's like the gentle roar of the ocean waves. Dallas Willard explains:

> The quality of God's voice is a matter of the *weight* or impact an impression makes on our consciousness. [It has] certain steady and calm force . . . inclines us toward assent. . . . We sense inwardly the immediate power of God's voice [and] the unquestionable authority. . . . It is a spirit of exalted peacefulness and confidence, of joy, of sweet reasonableness and of goodwill. It is, in short, the spirit

of Jesus [or] the overall tone and internal dynamics of his personal life as a whole. . . . It is this Spirit that marks the voice of God in our hearts. . . . And because his voice bears authority within itself, it does not need to be loud or hysterical.[21]

Teresa indicates that a genuine word from the Lord will typically surprise you, offer a world of meaning, bring clarity, imprint into your memory, and produce a living spark of faith that the word will come true.[22] She adds that divinely inspired experiences will also bring three jewels to you: knowledge of the greatness of God, self-knowledge that humbles you, and contempt for all earthly things except serving God.[23] That's the Spirit of truth marking you with tender love.[24]

Let's go back through the signs of genuine words or touches from the Spirit. Which ones have you experienced?

- Consistent with the Bible
- Calm authority
- Exalted peace and sweet reasonableness
- Gentle like the Spirit of Jesus
- Surprises you
- Offers a world of meaning
- Brings clarity
- Imprints into your memory
- Produces a living spark of faith
- Inspires you to worship God
- Humbles you
- Turns you away from worldly things

When you have a heavenly experience, you'll need discernment on whether God would have you keep it secret so you can marinate more in God's love, or if it's best to let your light shine so others can be drawn closer to Christ.[25] Also, it's important to remember that while special consolations from God are a bless-ing, they are *not* a sign of being a better Christ-follower. The true sign of a good life is *virtue*. In fact, Teresa points out that often it's *less mature* believers who receive supernatural touches in order to encourage their growth in Christ.[26] Spiritual consolations can occur in all of the CHRIST stages, or sometimes even before you put confidence in Christ. What's important in life—and central in the S Stage—is not getting a special touch of God but grow-ing in a conversational relationship with the Lord that helps us to enjoy and share the love of Christ with others. In the S Stage we don't seek God's blessings as much as we simply enjoy shar-ing with others the grace our Lord Jesus freely gives to all of us (Acts 20:35).

The Wounded Healer

The ancient Greek myth about the wounded healer expresses more surprising grace in the S Stage. Chiron (pronounced "Ky-ren") was a centaur, a mythical creature with the upper body of a human and the lower body of a horse. Most centaurs were savage, but Chiron had been civilized and tenderized by an incurable wound. His suffering motivated him to discover many medicines and to offer compassionate medical care for those who were sick or hurt-ing. Ironically, even though Chiron couldn't heal his own wound, people from around the world came to him at his home at the foot of Mount Pelion and were cured of their ailments. Carl Jung drew on this myth to teach, "Only the wounded physician heals. . . . The pains and burdens one bears and eventually overcomes are the source of great wisdom and healing power for others."[27]

Jesus is our Wounded Healer. The Son of God left heaven to be-come human and experience our needs, temptations, trials, pains, and injustices. From his wounds he ministers empathy and mercy to us (Heb. 4:15). The culmination of his ministry as the Wounded Healer was shedding his blood for us (Isa. 53:5; 1 Pet. 2:24). Recall that he could have called on his Father to dispatch legions of angels to deliver him from the cross, but instead he gladly chose *not* to save himself so he could save us.[28] Similarly, God did not heal Paul's thorn in the flesh but gave him an abundance of grace to endure his suffering with joy so he could minister comfort and encouragement to us as we go through hard times (2 Cor. 1:3–7; 12:7–10).

In God's service our wounds actually help to qualify us for ministry. The Spirit of Jesus takes our hurts and struggles that surfaced and were cared for in the I Stage and repurposes them in the S Stage. What does this look like? How can your wounds help you care for others? Henri Nouwen taught that wounded healers in the way of Jesus do not give analysis, advice, fixing, or reassurance. Instead, they give empathy by listening. Surprisingly, sometimes they also verbalize their own weaknesses and brokenness to the people they teach or care for. This is not dumping on others—it's giving them words for what they vaguely feel and encouraging them to reach out for Christ's comfort and grace.[29] In this ministry of divine hospitality "a shared pain is no longer paralyzing, but mobilizing."[30]

Anointed Ministry

The fullness of grace in the S Stage is portrayed by the Shepherd's oil that heals us becoming the oil that anoints us for ministry. The Beloved Disciple describes this as "an anointing from the Holy One" in which the Spirit of Jesus is our inner teacher and power source (1 John 2:20, 27). This is a main storyline in the Acts of the Apostles. At the beginning of Luke's second book, the resurrected King devotes forty days to weaning his disciples off his physical body and onto his Spirit by alternating between talking to them in the flesh and "through the Holy Spirit" (1:2). They learn to wait on Holy Spirit (Acts 1:4, 12–15) and act in "the Name" (5:41). In fact, thirty-four times they minister simply by speaking and acting in the name of Jesus, God's anointed one (4:26–27; 10:38). They find that this carries the anointing of his presence and power.

The disciples followed the Spirit of the Anointed One to make bold decisions like receiving into the church uncircumcised gentiles who didn't adhere to Judaism's strict interpretations of the law (15:1–21) and traveling overseas to bring the gospel to Europe (16:6–10). They were defined not by their doctrine but by their lifestyle of being Christlike, praising God and loving people even in persecution and suffering. So they became known as followers of "the Way" (9:2; 19:9, 23; 24:22).

Like the disciples in Acts, in the S Stage we operate by relying on Holy Spirit's power, not just our own thoughts, desires, or abilities. Jesus pointed out a poor widow who exemplifies this. She put just two cents in the temple offering, but this was more than the large offerings of the rich because only she gave with confidence in God (Mark 12:41–44). In other words, a lot from a person who has little dependence on God is not much, but a little bit from a person who is depending greatly on God is HUGE. Jesus is teaching us how to use Kingdom of God math!

Often anxiety is a sign that we're relying not on the Holy Spirit but on our own attempts to perform or feel in control. In my late twenties I (Bill) gave a keynote talk to two thousand people at a conference on recovery from addiction. As I stood on the platform and looked down at the sea of faces staring at me, I suddenly realized I was out over my skis going too fast downhill. My heart was racing, my stomach was doing somersaults, I was short of breath, and I was judging myself. Afterward, I decided I didn't want to be a public speaker!

Can you relate? How do you feel when you speak in front of a group? As many as 75 percent of people have a fear of public speaking.[31] In my case, afterward I prayed and processed my anxious emotions with Kristi, my therapist, and a friend. I decided to learn from my fall and get back on the mountain. I soaked myself in God's unconditional love to better learn how to base my self-esteem on my identity in Christ rather than my performance. Then I tried different ways of public speaking, including writing a manuscript. But what helped me the most was setting aside my script and practicing Jesus' teaching: "When you speak don't worry about what to say; put your trust in the Holy Spirit to speak" (Matt. 10:19, authors' paraphrase).

Later, I was trying to finish an article and had writer's block. Out of the blue, I heard God's voice in my mind saying, "Bill, the best words you write come *between the lines*." I stepped away from my computer and prayed, "That's right, Lord. You're the writer. I've been straining to work on this, but I want to trust the words you'll say to the reader." (That was also my prayer as I wrote the words you're reading now!)

Today I *enjoy* writing and speaking to large groups of people. If I feel anxious, I use it as a prompt to pray and put my confidence in the Spirit of Jesus to speak to people. I've learned that the wind of the Spirit is always blowing, and I just need to hoist my sails. That's what it's like to operate in the anointing of the Holy One.

An Easy Yoke

Jesus describes his nonanxious, Spirit-permeated, Spirit-powered way of life as serving in his easy yoke. I wrote a book on this because it's the theme of my life. In our Lord's analogy, he is the lead ox and we're the young ox. We get into the yoke with him in order to pull the plow across a field for planting and harvesting a crop of food that will feed hungry people. "Walk with me and work me," Jesus says. "Watch how I do it. Learn the unforced rhythms of grace. I won't lay anything heavy or ill-fitting on you. Keep company with me and you'll learn to live freely and lightly" (Matt. 11:29–30 MSG).

This yoke is Rabbi Jesus' teaching. But it's not just content— it's participating in the "unique Father-Son operation, coming out of Father and Son intimacies and knowledge" (Matt. 11:27 MSG). Jesus lived in a relaxed grace-yoke with his Father that empowered his ministry. For instance, he napped in his Abba's arms during a life-threatening storm at sea (Matt. 8:23–27), had compassion on the hungry people who interrupted his retreat (Matt. 14:13–14), and was silent and secure before his accusers (Mark 14:61).[32] In the yoke of intimacy with Jesus we are at ease and empowered.

But life is hard and unfair, you may be feeling. That's true. Jesus' easy yoke is not an easy life—it's an easy *way* of doing hard things. For instance, when God called us to start our Soul Shepherding nonprofit ministry, we resisted for a whole year. We were afraid to set aside our fee-for-service income as therapists and depend on people for donations, and we didn't know how to lead a nonprofit organization. Then, on a prayer hike in the hills near our home one day, I sensed the Lord saying, "Bill, there are people who would want to help you if you would let them." It was hard for us to step out in faith and ask people to partner with us, but it became a wonderful adventure of being led by the Spirit of Jesus.

Another time early in our ministry, we were on a mission trip, building houses for the poor near Tijuana, Mexico, and I was talking to a local pastor who had a dream to plant fifty churches in impoverished, rural neighborhoods. As we talked, I had a strong impression of the Spirit saying, "He needs Soul Shepherding. His pastor couples don't have access to what you know." For a variety of reasons, we didn't want a ministry in Mexico. Nonetheless, once we surrendered to the word of the sovereign Lord, we found that the Spirit of Jesus was with us and provided an easy way to do many hard things like fundraising, traveling back and forth across the border, and translating our talks and methods into Spanish. In eleven years of making multiple mission trips to offer retreats and training for pastors, we've seen the Lord bless us to be a blessing. Today there are over forty pastor couples with growing churches receiving ministry that is completely paid for by our donors.

The most important work we do in ministry situations like these is relying on the Spirit of God's unseen presence and power.

Jean-Pierre de Caussade, an eighteenth-century Jesuit priest, gave a beautiful description of the S Stage:

> The only condition necessary for this state of self-surrender is the present moment in which the soul, light as a feather, fluid as water, innocent as a child, responds to every movement of grace like a floating balloon. Such souls are like molten metal filling whatever vessel God chooses to pour them into.[33]

Wouldn't you like to be light, fluid, and fired up in your soul? You may want to try a few of these soul training practices:

- Submit your ambitions to God by praying, "Lord, please do not grant me more success or power than my character can handle."[34]
- Arrive early to a meeting or event in order to be prayerful.[35]
- Share a personal hurt or struggle with someone if it will help them be vulnerable and receive care.
- Whenever you feel jealous of people, pray for them to be blessed (because you've been blessed).
- Ask God to speak as you meditate on Scripture and then write down what the Spirit might be saying to you.
- Take a walk in your neighborhood and pray blessings on people you see.
- Abide in prayer to appreciate Christ's presence (see the soul care practice below).

················· **Trail Markers for the S Stage** ·················

AGE	Usually 40+ (if ever)
FAITH	Venture on God
COGNITIVE DEVELOPMENT	Integrating paradoxes and transcending limits
ROADBLOCK & TEMPTATIONS	Dark Night of the Soul Blurring emotion and the Spirit Impulsiveness (lack self-discipline, devalue planning) Diminishing the importance of the Bible Believing you're better than other people (pride) Disillusionment with church
IMAGES OF GOD	Holy Spirit as Friend, Guide, and Advocate
GRACE	Surprise blessings to share
LESSONS	Waiting/relying on God's presence and power Loving God in a Dark Night of the Soul Hearing God's voice (and mystical experiences) Being unhurried and nonanxious in stress Living and working in Jesus' easy yoke Serving as a wounded healer for others
SPIRITUAL DISCIPLINES	Watching and praying to act with Holy Spirit Abandoning outcomes to God Listening to God in Scripture and daily life Listening to people with empathy Abiding in prayer for self and others Secrecy (doing good deeds without recognition) Fixed-hour prayer to integrate prayer and work Allowing margin to be unhurried Blessing "competitors"
CHURCH MINISTRIES	Spiritual friendship Spiritual direction Spiritual retreats

············ **Guidebook Scriptures for the S Stage** ············

- **Jesus' easy yoke is powerful:** "Come to me. . . . I'll show you how to take a real rest. Walk with me and work with me—watch how I do it. Learn the unforced rhythms of grace" (Matt. 11:28–29 MSG).

- **You can be anointed and empowered:** "You will receive power when the Holy Spirit comes on you; and you will be my witnesses" (Acts 1:8).

- **Follow the Spirit of Jesus:** "Since we live by the Spirit, let us keep in step with the Spirit" (Gal. 5:25).

- **Pray before acting:** "Wait until you hear a sound like troops marching through the tops of the trees. . . . That sound will mean I have marched out ahead of you" (2 Sam. 5:24 CEV).

- **Learn to love God in a Dark Night of the Soul:** "How long, LORD? Will you forget me forever? How long will you hide your face from me? . . . But I trust in your unfailing love; my heart rejoices in your salvation. I will sing the LORD's praise, for he has been good to me" (Ps. 13:1, 5–6).

- **Wounded healers bless others:** "[The] God of all healing counsel . . . comes alongside us when we go through hard times, and before you know it, he brings us alongside someone else who is going through hard times so that we can be there for that person just as God was there for us" (2 Cor. 1:3–4 MSG).

- **Enjoy new freedom:** "[The Lord] brought me out into a spacious place" (Ps. 18:19).

Soul Care Practice

Centering in Christ

Years ago, when I (Bill) was meeting with Ray Ortlund Sr. for spiritual direction, he turned me on to his favorite author, Thomas Kelly, a Quaker educator and missionary from Ohio who lived early in the twentieth century. For three years before Kelly died at just age forty-eight, he met with a small group of his students to read, discuss, and pray through the spiritual classics. He became "Light-centered," "wholly God-enthralled," and "God-intoxicated!"[36] In 1941, shortly after his untimely death, four of his essays were published as *A Testament of Devotion*. It became a classic like the books that ignited his own revival.

Ray read Kelly's book, and it inspired his own bestselling book *Lord, Make My Life a Miracle!* He effused, "I read a sentence from Thomas Kelly that set my heart on fire. He prayed, 'Lord, make my life a miracle!' Oh, God! That's it! You're the original Miracle, and I live in You. Why shouldn't my life be a miracle? Why shouldn't I be able to show others how to be miracles?"[37] Ray elaborated to me over lunch, "When I die I want people to look at my life and say, 'Look what God did! That had to be God. Ray couldn't have done that!'" Sure enough, I celebrated the miracle of Ray's life with eight hundred people, including over four hundred pastors who had been in his discipleship groups. Like the great Quaker before him, he had gathered leaders in small groups so that together they might fan into flame their love for Christ.

The hope of my life becoming a miracle like Ray's inspired me to read Kelly's devotional classic. I read it straight through, kneeling in prayer for three hours at my ancient, tear-stained prayer bench. Then I spent a fourth hour facedown on the floor in silence, praying that my life would be explained not by my abilities and work but by the activity of the Spirit of Jesus. That day I believe that something from Kelly's heart for God got into me.

But whenever I tell this story Kristi interjects, "You don't have to kneel or get on your face for hours like Bill did. I went to the beach to read Kelly's book and pray, and it had a profound impact on me!"

"Jesus, Be the Center"

I'd like to share with you one of my favorite excerpts from Kelly. He helps us to be still and tune in to the Breath of Life within:

> We feel the pull of many obligations and try to fulfill them all.
> We are unhappy, uneasy, strained, oppressed, and fearful we shall be shallow. For over the margins of life comes a whisper, a faint call, a premonition of richer living which we know we are passing by. Strained by the very mad pace of our daily outer burdens . . . strained by an inward uneasiness . . . we have hints that there is a way of life vastly richer and deeper than all this hurried existence, a life of unhurried serenity and peace and power.
> If only we could slip over into that Center! If only we could find the Silence which is the source of sound! We have known some people who seem to have found this deep Center of living. . . .
> We have not counted this Holy Thing within us to be the most precious thing in the world. We have not surrendered *all else*, to attend to it alone.[38]

Let's pause and take a minute to be quiet in "the Silence which is the source of sound" and *behold Christ transfigured in our hearts.* We can meditate on a Scripture phrase to "center down," as Ray liked to say.

- Repeat this prayer of the heart slowly and gently: "Jesus, be the Center" (inspired by Matt. 17:8 NLT).[39]
- Pray for a specific situation or person: "Jesus, be the Center for _____."
- Rest in the presence and prayers of Holy Spirit.

Soul Talk

1. What is one thing you learned about the Dark Night of the Soul?
2. Which distinguishing marks of a genuine word or vision from God are most helpful to you?
3. What does it look like for you to do your work or ministry in Jesus' easy yoke or as a wounded healer?
4. What is a spiritual discipline for the S Stage that you'd like to experiment with? How do you hope this will help you?
5. How were you encouraged by reading the Spirit-Led Ministry Scriptures and abiding in the prayer "Jesus, be the Center"?

Packing List for the T Stage

The culmination of the journey of the soul is Transforming Union. To experience this stage of faith you'll need:

1. Desire for union with Jesus
2. Practices of contemplative prayer
3. Christ's compassion for all people
4. Habits for appreciating the Trinity with you

The T Stage:
Transforming Union

Our journey of the soul culminates with being united in the love of Jesus Christ.

> Surely goodness and mercy shall follow me all the
>   days of my life;
> And I will dwell in the house of the LORD forever.
>
> Psalm 23:6 NKJV

I (Kristi) used to feel that the classic devotional authors were totally out of my league. When I read their life stories and writings I sank into shame: *I'm not that devoted to God. I'm not serving as a missionary or doing a great work. I haven't had mystical experiences like that, and I'm terrified to suffer. I wish I could be so loving for Jesus and the people he died for.* Other times I'd secretly roll my eyes and think, *Oh please, that's so holier-than-thou.*

So when Bill asked me to write this book with him, I didn't feel worthy and I initially declined. Later, when I prayed about it, I was surprised to sense the Lord calling me to write by speaking to my heart the word "surrender." I told you about hearing that word at a conference years ago and freezing in fear, as if God were holding a surgeon's scalpel. But this time I appreciated Jesus' smile, which inspired my trust and obedience. Now I see it as ironic that the Lord led me to coauthor this book with Bill after having led him to coauthor our young children with me!

My experience with taking courage to step out into the Lord's call for me illustrates that our journey with Jesus is one of increasing submission to God. The life of devotion culminates in this final CHRIST stage of Transforming Union.

As I write to you now, it's in the spirit of Teresa of Jesus' prayer: *May it please His Majesty to guide the writing Bill and I do in order to help you understand this most glorious mansion of union with the Bridegroom of our soul. I pray that God's mercies would not be hidden to you, so that together we can bring greater praise and glory to the name of Jesus Christ.*[1]

Characteristics of the T Stage

Psalm 23 ends on a high note: "Your beauty and love chase after me every day of my life. I'm back home in the house of GOD for the rest of my life" (v. 6 MSG). In the beginning of our journey the Shepherd was directive to *make* us lie down in green pastures, *lead* us beside still waters, and *guide* us in the good path. Then, in the dark valley of death when we thought he'd abandoned us, we found that he was *with* us each step of the way. Now at the T Stage he *follows* us. On our journey we've incorporated the graces of earlier stages and grown in the character of Christ.

In the T Stage our total focus is to bring glory to God by loving all the people we can. We live by Jesus' teachings and Holy Spirit's voice, so our Father gives us space and freedom for what we want to do with our lives. It's like he hands us the keys to his new car and nods, "Go ahead. Take it for a drive!" The Lord trusts *you* and wants to empower you to do what you want.[2] *With the Spirit of Jesus beating in your heart and breathing in your lungs you can do great things to love people and advance the Kingdom of God on earth today!*

This last stage of emotional and spiritual growth is union with the cosmic Christ. It's the oneness with Love that we all long for. Many people experience touches of this, but few actually live in it.[3] For those who do, it's usually not until age sixty or older. The feeling of divine union is elusive. Yet Teresa describes this last mansion not as far away but as "an abiding-place" *in our soul* for His Majesty, Jesus, to create for us a "second heaven" that glows with light and love. Here the Most Holy Trinity of Father, Son, and Spirit is revealed to us, individually and collectively. She says our growing intimacy with the Three-in-One fosters wonder, happy companionship, alertness, rest, assurance that we're never alone, and the capacity to love others well, even in business worries and numerous trials.[4]

The T Stage's contagious life of love correlates with Fowler's last stage of Universalizing Faith. You have compassion for *all* people and welcome whoever you can into your expanding community. It's to be prepared to subvert any person, organization, or religion that blocks the flow of free grace to everyone. It's to be truly and fully human.[5] Erikson, in his last stage of psychosocial development, calls this *Integrity*. We've come to accept the gift of our life on earth as divine image bearers for others, rather than sliding into regrets over all that we didn't get to do in life.[6] We're aging with grace, learning to appreciate our wrinkles and sags as signs of being used up in the service of our Savior and Lord. We're at peace with dying, ready to be led by Jesus into heaven.

Probably the best way to understand this last and mysterious stage of faith is to consider examples of people who have lived it:

* Madame Guyon (1592–1663) was rejected by her husband, children, and church, but she showed the poor and uneducated in France how to experience the deep love of Christ.[7]

- Brother Lawrence (1614–1691), also from France, was a lame kitchen helper with little talent and lots of shame, but he learned to practice God's presence continually, even in the noise and clatter of the monastery kitchen. His story blessed millions of people.[8]
- Frank Laubach (1884–1970) was a Christian missionary from New York to the Philippines who kept failing till he heard God challenge him to teach illiterate Muslims how to read. He discovered that "everything is bathed in God. I swim in God as a fish in the sea."[9] (See his story below.)
- Corrie ten Boom (1892–1983) was an assistant watchmaker in the Netherlands who was afraid of the Nazis but took courage to hide Jews in her home.
- Mother Teresa (1910–1997) was a simple nun from Albania who had compassion and cheerful hospitality for the poor who were dying right outside her window in the streets of Calcutta, India. (See her story below.)
- Martin Luther King Jr. (1929–1968) was an ordinary pastor in Atlanta, Georgia, who rose up to defend African Americans against racial injustice.

Path Finder for the T Stage

For each statement below, circle T if it's true of your current experience with God:

YOUR CURRENT EXPERIENCE WITH GOD	TRUE?
1. I rely on Holy Spirit's presence with me as I do whatever I'm doing.	T
2. In simple and meaningful ways, I enjoy the presence of the Trinity.	T
3. I seek to be devoted to Jesus Christ and indifferent to everything else.	T
4. I appreciate God's love for other people, whatever their religion.	T
5. Often I'm able to bless those who curse me, and God takes care of me.	T

YOUR CURRENT EXPERIENCE WITH GOD	TRUE?
6. I want to share more spiritual depth than most people I interact with.	T
7. I'm fine with suffering or death as long as I'm united with Christ.	T
8. I often enjoy praying quietly with few words, offering my heart to abide in the Spirit.	T

If you circled "true" more often for the T Stage than the other CHRIST stages, this may be your home stage.

Roadblock: Diminishing Jesus Christ

Teresa of Jesus says the key that opens the door to abiding in the Trinity as our home is appreciating the humanity of Jesus and his love relationship with the Father (John 15:9; 17:20–21).[10] Think about it. Jesus Christ is the eternal Son of God, the co-creator of the universe, the radiance of God's glory and exact portrait of God, and the one who sustains all things by his powerful word (Heb. 1:1–4). Yet he smiles and calls us his friends (John 15:15). His Papa is your Papa and his Spirit is your life. Here we're looking to Jesus of Nazareth as *the first disciple of Yahweh* who models for us how to do it. Paul refers to this as developing the faith "*of* Christ" (Gal. 2:20 YLT, emphasis added). Notice how we're keeping the humanity of Jesus connected to his divinity.

Tragically, radical grace and open-mindedness at the T Stage mislead some Christians to lose touch with the preciousness and glory of the Son of God. Or perhaps it's because they've become bored with the familiarity of their faith. It's disappointing when a Christian speaker or author rarely mentions Jesus or treats him like he's just a great moral teacher. In contrast, recall how the apostle Paul enthralls our minds and hearts with the supremacy of Jesus Christ in all things, pointing to Christ once every ten seconds in his thirteen-minute message (see the soul care practice for chapter 7).[11] In healthy T-Stage spirituality, we keep drawing on and sharing with others the graces of the previous stages, starting with the C Stage's sticky-love bond with Jesus. (Recall that we said the CHRIST stages are cyclical, not linear.)

Ironically, another way you may diminish Christ in the T Stage is by neglecting yourself as made in God's image. If the enemy can tempt you to disregard your own needs and worth, then he can sabotage your soul and influence for Christ. The twelfth-century church father Bernard of Clairvaux speaks to this temptation with surprising wisdom by identifying the highest degree of love to be self-love for God's sake.[12] In true Christlikeness, you realize that caring for yourself is part of loving God and others because they want you to be cared for. It also enables you to sustain your life of service without burning out.

Grace: Practicing God's Presence

Trinitarian prayer is the heart of the T Stage. Somewhere we heard a humorous story about the blessing and power of praying to the Triune God. There were three simple monks who lived by a simple prayer to God: "We are three; you are Three. Have mercy on us. Amen." Miracles sometimes happened when they prayed this way. When the bishop heard about their informal prayer life, he was concerned and traveled by ship to their island. He instructed them in proper prayer and sailed back home, pleased with himself. From his ship, he saw a huge ball of light skimming over the ocean. It got closer and closer. It was the three hermits dancing on the water! They stepped off the ocean and onto the ship and in unison said to the bishop, "We are so sorry, but we have forgotten your teaching on prayer. Please remind us." The bishop replied in meekness, "Forget everything I have taught you and continue to pray in your old way!"

This is a picture of the Father, Son, and Spirit relating in a continual *dance of love* in which each thrills to shine a spotlight on the others, as if to say, "Now you lead the dance."[13] The Father beams on Jesus and declares, "You are my Son, whom I love; with you I am well pleased" (Mark 1:11). Jesus praises, "My Father . . . is greater than all" (John 10:29). The Son always submits to his Father, and the Father always draws people to his Son (John 5:19; 6:44). Holy Spirit keeps crying out, "Abba, Father!" (Gal. 4:6) and "Jesus is Lord!" (1 Cor. 12:3). Father gives us Holy Spirit as his special gift (Acts 1:5). Jesus stands up for Holy Spirit: "Don't ever speak a word against Parakletos" (Luke 12:10, authors' paraphrase). Holy Spirit wants to be known as "the Spirit of Jesus" and keeps reminding us of things Jesus said (John 14:26; Acts 16:7; Phil. 1:19).

Don't you want to join the dance? It's beautiful how the Holy, Holy, Holy immerse us in their intimate and glorious community (Matt. 11:27; John 17:22). The Son graces us, the Father loves us, and the Spirit companions us (2 Cor. 13:14). We become the Trinity's temple for others to experience God's presence (1 Cor. 6:19). We're learning to "Rejoice always, pray continually, [and] give thanks in all circumstances" (1 Thess. 5:16–18). Instead of worrying about the future or feeling guilty about the past, we're enjoying the present with the Spirit of Jesus.

In Romans 12 Paul spells out that practicing God's presence is a matter of continually loving people in practical ways. In view of God's mercy to us, we offer our bodies to serve others. We humbly offer our gifts to help people in our community. With sincere love, we turn away from evil and seek to do what is good. We honor others above self. We serve the Lord with zeal, joyful hope, patience in trials, and faithfulness in prayer. We share with God's people who are in need and we practice hospitality. We bless those who persecute us. We rejoice with people's good fortune and empathize with their difficulties to live in harmony with them. We set aside our pride and associate happily with people of low position (vv. 1–16).

In the T Stage, practicing God's presence becomes less of a *practice* and more of a habitual, natural, and unconscious reliance on Holy Spirit. Often we find ourselves praising God or breathing a prayer when we hadn't intended to do so. This is not ethereal or idyllic but quite practical. As we go about our daily work and interact with people, we do so with the Spirit of Jesus and for God's glory.

Not of This World

To experience the Trinity and live in their fellowship of generous love is "not of this world" (John 18:36). Yet it's normal for Christ-followers. In the New Testament, Peter had a vision from God while praying on a rooftop (Acts 10:9–16), Lydia and her friends met the Spirit of Christ by the river in Philippi (Acts 16:13–15), and Paul was caught up in the third heaven (2 Cor. 12:2–5). In this book we've shared some of our spiritual graces from God, along with those of devotional authors and personal friends of ours. Perhaps you too have received a word or touch from God?

If you've had a mystical experience, you may be sheepish about it after finding that some people think it's weird. But the New Testament uses the Greek word *musterion* twenty-seven times to indicate "a secret revealed by God" or "mystical truth."[14] For instance, in 1 Corinthians 2, Paul writes about "the mystery of God" that he personally received and shared with others so generously (v. 7). He indicates that these mystical revelations are wonderful blessings that Holy Spirit sometimes gives us. Yet they seem foolish to human wisdom. It's only spiritual people who are able to receive these spiritual gifts from God (vv. 12–16). Paul, like Peter and Lydia before him, received mysterious blessings from heaven and was strengthened to love God and others better.

Pastor and Bible teacher A. W. Tozer insists, "Any genuine, personal relationship with Christ is mystical because he no longer walks on the earth in bodily form. It's the breathless awe that a true worshiper feels in the presence of a holy God."[15] He says Christian mysticism is simply experiencing faith down in the depths of feeling, walking the high road of truth, living in a world of spiritual reality, and being "quietly, deeply, and sometimes almost ecstatically aware of the Presence of God in [our] own nature and in the world around [us]."[16]

In the later stages of faith we set our affections on Christ above, deny ourselves worldly pleasures and honors, and live to love all people for his sake (Col. 3:1–17). We become like aliens in this world (Heb. 11:13). "Two roads diverged in a yellow wood," and we chose the road less traveled.[17] Even among many Christians we may feel like we don't fit in. Unlike the broader Christian culture, we may appreciate quiet, simplicity, being unhurried, nondual thinking, and salvation as eternal living, not just a transaction of forgiveness. Tozer describes the feeling of being a lonely pilgrim:

> The truly spiritual [person] is indeed something of an oddity. You live not for yourself but to promote the interests of Another. . . . You find few who care to talk about that which is the supreme object of your interest, so you're often silent and preoccupied. . . .
> It is this very loneliness that throws you back upon God. "Though my father and mother forsake me, the Lord will receive me" (Psalm 27:10). . . . You learn in inner solitude what you could not have learned in the crowd—that Christ is All in all [Col. 3:11] . . . that in Him we have and possess life's *summum bonum* [the supreme good from which all other good is derived].[18]

If you long for intimacy with Jesus, hear God's voice, enjoy contemplative prayer, and see the Holy Mystery in all things and all people, then some First Half believers will think you're New Age or heretical. You may be persecuted by religious people who feel threatened or offended by your spirituality and inclusiveness. This was the case for many of the Lord's most devoted and loving servants throughout history, including those we mentioned earlier in this chapter. Recall that our Founder warned us, "If the world hates you, keep in mind that it hated me first" (John 15:18). Mature disciples in the T Stage find honor in learning to be joyfully faithful to love Jesus and his bride (the church) during persecution and trials.

Mysticism and Mission

Frank Laubach's life and writings embody the Christlike characteristics of Transforming Union. He integrates prayer and work in practical, nonascetic ways. He's at once a mystic and a missionary, loving God and loving people. He's like Mary sitting at Yeshua's[19] feet, with her soul hanging on his every word, *and* he's like Martha busy in the kitchen, serving her Master and Messiah by preparing food for her guests (Luke 10:38–42). But, as is usually the case, it took many years for Laubach to discover the expansive open country of the later CHRIST stages.

In the 1930s Laubach was a middle-aged missionary from New York City serving on Mindanao Island in the Philippines. In fifteen years of labor he felt he had failed to reach the local Muslims with Christ's love. He was in poor health, lonely, and depressed. He had lost three of his four children to malaria. Then he failed to become president of a seminary in Manila by *one vote*—his own ballot cast for the other candidate who won.[20] He was in desolation at The Wall, languishing in what seemed like many wasted years and wondering, *Where is God in all this? What should I do with my life now?*

Each day he took his dog Tip with him for a prayer walk up Signal Hill, which overlooks the giant Lake Lanao and endless cottage homes in the valley below. One day he prayed:

> "Look at these Moros down there around the lake. I've wanted to help them since I first heard of them [thirty years ago]. But they are ignorant and dirty. They chew betel nuts. They are thieves and murderers. What can I do with them?" Suddenly it seemed that God was speaking to him through his own lips. "My child!" the words came clearly, "the Moros don't like you because you don't really like them. You have failed because you don't really love them. You feel superior to them because you are white. If you can forget you are an American and think only of how I love them, they will respond. . . . If you want the Moros to be fair to your religion, be fair to theirs. Study the Koran with them."[21]

Laubach gave up his prejudices and met with the Moro leaders to learn their holy book, language, and customs, and they became friends. That kind of open-minded, nonsectarian, accepting attitude is typical of T-Stage disciples of Christ: they are happy to glean wisdom from Muslims, Buddhists, atheist scientists, New Age artists, fundamentalist Christians, or hip-hop rappers. At the same time Laubach poured out his soul to love his new Muslim friends, he engaged in a vigorous spiritual experiment of filling every minute with thoughts of God.[22] As a modern mystic, he found that serving the needs of other people greatly helped him to practice God's presence.

"Frankie," as Dallas Willard sometimes affectionately called him, wrote letters home to his father in New York about his personal experiences in prayer and caring for the Moros:

> I have started out trying to live all my waking moments in conscious listening to the inner voice, asking without ceasing, "What Father do you desire said? What Father, do you desire done this minute?" It is clear that this is exactly what Jesus was doing all day every day. But it is not what His followers have been doing in very large numbers. . . .
>
> I am feeling God in each movement, by an act of will—willing that He shall direct these fingers that now strike this typewriter—willing that He shall pour through my steps as I walk—willing that He shall direct my words as I speak, and my very jaw as I eat! . . .
>
> It is exactly this "moment by moment," every waking moment, surrender, responsiveness, obedience, sensitiveness, pliability, "lost in his love," that I now have the mind-bent to explore with all my might. It means two burning passions: First, to be like Jesus. Second, to respond to God as a violin responds to the bow of the master.
>
> In defense of my opening my soul and laying it bare to the public gaze in this fashion, I may say that it seems to me that we really seldom do anybody much good except as we share the deepest experiences of our souls. . . . I disapprove of the usual practice of talking "small talk" . . . we need to struggle for more richness of soul. As for me, I am convinced that this spiritual pilgrimage is infinitely

worthwhile, the most important thing I know of to talk about. . . . And how I hunger for others to tell me their soul adventures![23]

Much to Frankie's surprise, his letters became a classic book of devotion to Christ. His focus was on serving the Moros by teaching them to read. By listening to God's voice and relying on the assistance of the Spirit of Jesus, he developed an innovative method of literacy training for them. He translated a retelling of the gospel of Jesus, as well as oral stories of heroes from their culture, and they relished reading these. He also provided medical care, parenting guidance, and agricultural training. Then they came to love and respect Jesus and many came to Laubach's church. The Moros became so friendly that for the first time in three centuries visitors felt safe to travel there.[24]

The great success Laubach had with the Moros opened the door for him to provide literacy training throughout the Philippines and ultimately around the world. During his lifetime he consulted with kings, presidents, and other leaders from many nations, and his program taught 60 million illiterate people to read.[25]

A Divine Partnership

Frank Laubach's spirituality and influence may seem out of reach to you. But Frankie insisted he was just an ordinary man serving God. Dallas Willard personally said the same thing to me (Bill), and he demonstrated this repeatedly with his humility and vulnerability. This can encourage our faith that God wants to do more through my life and your life than we could ask or imagine (Eph. 3:20). In the T Stage you come to deeply believe in God's special purpose for your life, so you expand your loving concerns to ever-widening circles of people, including those who are very different from you.

Yet you may not want a life like Laubach's. From one perspective, his life seems hard. Until the day he died at age eighty-five, he worked his fingers to the bone to translate the love of Christ

into the language of illiterate people groups around the world. He
suffered so much, and he gave up so much that he could've enjoyed
in the world. But he would not say his life was hard. He had great
joy and strength in Jesus, even in stress and pain (which come to
all of us in various ways). The distinguishing mark of his life that
is so worthy of aspiration and emulation is that it was an increasingly supernatural, blessed, and fruitful union with the resurrected
Christ. He shows us the power of an ordinary person's life *happily
abandoned* to the Kingdom of Light and Love.

In another letter home to his dad, Frankie explained his delightful and successful partnership with Holy Spirit. This is the life we
all want. It's a great example of living and working in Jesus' easy
yoke in the S and T Stages:

> I feel simply carried along each hour, doing my part in a plan which
> is far beyond myself. The sense of cooperation with God in little
> things is what so astonishes me, for I have never felt this way be-
> fore. I need something, and turn around to find it waiting for me.
> I must work, to be sure, but there is God working along with me.
> To know this gives a sense of security and assurance for the future
> which is also new to my life. I seem to have to make sure of only
> one thing now, and . . . God takes care of all the rest. My part is to
> *live this hour in continuous inner conversation with God and in perfect
> responsiveness to His will, to make this hour gloriously rich.*[26]

Fourth Water Spirituality

Teresa of Jesus' analogy of the Four Waters illustrates the progression and benefits of learning to depend on the presence of the
Spirit with us.

First Water

In the beginning of our journey with Jesus in the C and H Stages,
we get a bucket to draw up water from a well and then carry that

water one bucketful at a time to our home and the plants in our garden. Back and forth we go to satisfy our thirst. We have to work hard to grow in our discipleship to Christ.

Second Water

In the R Stage we get smarter and build a waterwheel system. We crank the wheel and water runs through an aqueduct and flows as a stream into our garden or the gardens of other people. We're using our gifts to help more and more people drink the living water of God's Spirit, though it still requires a lot of human power to maintain the aqueduct and keep cranking the wheel.

No Water

At The Wall we run out of water. We crank the waterwheel, but no water flows except a trickle that barely keeps us alive. We go back to our bucket and drop it down the well, but it's empty. Suffering, overworking, doubts, or a Dark Night of the Soul can leave us in a dry season with no rain in sight. Dealing with confusion, emotional distress, and spiritual desolation saps our energy, especially if we deny these emotions.

Third Water

In the I Stage we use a new water source. We find a spring on a hill and build an outflowing stream so that the river of the Spirit can flow downhill into the garden of our soul. Using the natural spring water and power of gravity means we have a flow of water for ourselves and the people we care for with *much less effort* than when we had to crank the wheel or carry buckets in the previous stages.

Fourth Water

In the S and T Stages we pray for rain and God sends a gentle rainfall or refreshing mist. This is the optimal way to water the garden of our soul because it requires the least effort and strain, and the rain makes our gardens verdant green and abundantly fruitful. In these final phases of spiritual maturity our works of love are not self-generated—they're a *response* to the Spirit's gracious initiative and power.[27]

The way A. W. Tozer wrote *The Pursuit of God* illustrates Fourth Water spirituality. One night in 1948 he took a red-eye train from Chicago to preach in Texas. The porter brought him a table and pulled the curtain on his roomette, and it became a sanctuary for a fourteen-hour vigil of prayer and writing. With nothing but his Bible, pen, paper, and the Holy Spirit, he wrote one of the greatest masterpieces of devotion to Christ in one sitting![28] Often our best work for God comes as a spontaneous overflowing of grace from our heart.

Mother Teresa is another example of Fourth Water spirituality. Her tireless compassion for the poorest of the poor dying alone in the streets of Calcutta left her soul parched dry in a fifty-year-long Dark Night, yet living waters kept flowing from her prayers, smile, and hands to the destitute. It seems she lived at The Wall while remaining in the T Stage, united with the compassion of Christ. Her tireless faithfulness to share the mercy of Jesus deeply impacted countless people around the world.[29]

Abiding in Christ for Others

It would be great if we all had a friend or mentor in the T Stage because it helps us to grasp this life of transcendent union with Christ and to know it's really possible. As we've indicated, Dallas Willard provided this living model of a Christ-life for Kristi and me. One day during his class at the monastery, I was in my room reading at my desk when I noticed him outside my window, strolling in the rose garden with his hands behind his back and humming a hymn. In class later that same day, another student got testy and critical. Dallas put his hands behind his back as he had in the garden and responded to the angry student with a warm smile, gentle listening, curious questions, and affirmation.

Dallas' bodily demeanor while being publicly criticized was just as cheerful and content as when he was smelling roses and humming a favorite hymn. Instead of using his PhD to put this snippy student in his place, he lovingly served him. When the student felt understood and respected, his boiling pot simmered down. Furthermore, Dallas himself was freed from the burden of anger or wounded pride. Prior to this challenge, outside the spotlight of his lectern, he had trained himself in the teachings of Jesus so that he was prepared to offer kind words and generous service to others, including people who disrespected or mistreated him. *In the garden and then in the classroom Dallas was abiding in Christ's love for himself and his students.*

Can you imagine being that nondefensive and generous-spirited with someone who publicly criticizes you? Without going into anxiety, anger, shame, or people-pleasing? In the New Testament we see many ordinary people entering into a divine life in the Kingdom of the Heavens in which they are able to be loving, joyful, and peaceful in tribulations. We can learn to do the same. In his first letter the apostle Peter encourages us that by being sprinkled with the blood of Jesus Christ and trusting in his resurrection (1:2–3) we can become increasingly "saturated with an ecstatic joy, indescribably sublime and immersed in glory," full of sincere love for one another, free of deceit and jealousy and slander, and free of worries because you know that "[God] always tenderly cares for you" (1:8, 22; 2:1; 5:7 TPT).

Truly, the T Stage is just the beginning of the Transfigured One bringing out the best in you. The wondrous love relationship you'll experience with the Bridegroom of your soul in the eternal glory of heaven is far better than anything you've ever seen, heard, or imagined during your life on earth! (See 1 Cor. 2:7–9.)

Yet, in Dallas' words, we can begin to enter the divine world *now* if we take small steps into "the way of pervasive inner transformation." He insists, "All of the hindrances to our putting off the old person and putting on the new one can be removed or mastered. And that will enable us to walk increasingly in the wholeness, holiness, and power of the Kingdom of the Heavens. No one need live in spiritual and personal defeat. A life of victory over sin and circumstance is accessible to all."[30]

Dallas is describing a life of love. *We're marrying contemplative prayer and compassionate action.* This requires developing bodily habits for tuning in to and depending on the Breath of Life's immanent presence, prayers, and power that sustain us to be the heart and hands of Jesus to other people. For instance, here are some small steps to cultivate T-Stage agape:

- Look at people around you as you silently pray, "Christ is all, and is in all" (Col. 3:11).
- Attend church (even if you feel you don't benefit much) because your participation blesses God and the community.
- Practice yoga poses while breathing praises to God and intercessions for people.
- Enjoy a poem, painting, or music to appreciate God's beauty and bless an artist.
- Be still and contemplate God (Ps. 46:1) in a dark closet for ten minutes (or more) as you seek to release all thoughts and offer your heart to Christ alone.
- When someone mistreats you, secretly pray blessings on them.
- Consecrate your whole person to love the Trinity and your neighbor (see the soul care practice below).

Trail Markers for the T Stage

AGE	Usually not till 60+ (if ever)
FAITH	Integrity
COGNITIVE DEVELOPMENT	Universalizing compassion for all
ROADBLOCK & TEMPTATIONS	Diminishing Jesus Christ (the God-man)
	Not participating in church
	Neglecting personal needs
	Judging people who seek consolation
	Ethereal "spirituality" (contemplation without action)
	Getting depressed over feeling odd or lonely
IMAGES OF GOD	Jesus as Bridegroom
	The Trinity (Father, Son, and Spirit as One God)
GRACE	Practicing God's presence
LESSONS	Devotion to love and honor Jesus Christ in all things
	Relating to the Trinity
	Being a pilgrim and stranger in the world
	Welcoming diverse people into your enlarging community
	Serving difficult people and enemies
	Dying with integrity (not despair) and ready for heaven
SPIRITUAL DISCIPLINES	Turning activity into prayer (embodying God's Word)
	Contemplative prayer (remaining in quiet prayer)
	Appreciating the Trinity
	Staying engaged in church and community
	Blessing those who mistreat you
	Prayers of consecration
	Sacrifices of love (even in spiritual dryness)
	Rejoicing in Christ during persecution and trials
CHURCH MINISTRIES	Loving, prayerful presence to all

············· Guidebook Scriptures for the T Stage ·············

- **The Trinity is your home:** Jesus prayed for us, "As you are in me, Father, and I am in you . . . may they be in us so that the world will believe you sent me. I have given them the glory you gave me, so they may be one as we are one" (John 17:21–22 NLT).
- **We're strangers on earth:** "Friends, this world is not your home, so don't make yourselves cozy in it. Don't indulge your ego at the expense of your soul" (1 Pet. 2:11 MSG).
- **Continually appreciate God's presence:** "I have set the LORD always before me; because he is at my right hand, I shall not be shaken" (Ps. 16:8 ESV).
- **Be kind to all people:** "Do your best to live as everybody's friend" (Rom. 12:18 TPT).
- **Bless difficult people:** "Love your enemies and pray for those who mistreat you. That's what your Father in the heavens does for you and for all people, and it's how you show that you are his children" (Matt. 5:44–45, authors' paraphrase).
- **Passionately unite with Jesus Christ:** "I want to know Christ—yes, to know the power of his resurrection and participation in his sufferings, becoming like him in his death, and so, somehow, attaining to the resurrection from the dead" (Phil. 3:10–11).
- **Be ready to die:** "For to me, to live is Christ and to die is gain" (Phil. 1:21).

Soul Care Practice

Consecration Prayer

The shepherd-king David is described in the Bible as a man after God's own heart (Acts 13:22). His prayers of devotion fill the Psalms and are there for us to take heart from (as we discussed in chapter 7).[31] Repeatedly in the Psalter we see that when David was treated unjustly, he didn't seek revenge but submitted to his Sovereign, set his heart's passion on his Lover, and prayed for his enemies. That is the spirit of the T Stage.

Like many of God's great ones through history, John Wesley penned a prayer of total dedication to love the Lord and his neighbors, and this inspired his spiritual renewal and ongoing life in the Spirit:

O Lord, may nothing dwell in my soul
But your pure love alone.
Till my every thought, word, and act be love.
Yes, Lord, may your love possess me whole;
You're my joy, my treasure, my crown![32]

A consecration prayer is helpful at all of the CHRIST stages. Wesley was probably in the Inner Journey stage when he penned his prayer. In this final stage of Transforming Union we embody our prayer of consecration in a life of love that engages our *whole being*.

Lifting Up Your Soul to the Trinity

In Psalm 63 David prays with his entire self, using each of his personality functions to love God and others. Then in Psalm 86 he offers his soul to Adonai with a simple prayer of the heart: "O Lord, encircle me, for I love you.... To you I lift up my soul" (vv. 1–4, authors' paraphrase).

Here are some steps to use David's prayer to lift up your whole person to God in a life of devoted love:

1. Pray with David: "O Lord, encircle me, for I love you.... To you I lift up my soul." (To do this as a breath prayer you can breathe in the first half and breathe out the second half.)
2. Repeat the prayer, replacing "soul" with each personality function below.
3. As you pray, engage your body in prayer by using the suggested hand motions:
   - Heart (touch your physical heart)
   - Mind (touch your head)
   - Feelings (touch your stomach)
   - Body (make a muscle with your arms)
   - Social connections (move your hands in from your chest and out toward your social environment)
   - Soul (bring your hands down toward your waist and lift them up and out like a fountain)
4. Offer your prayer to the Trinity: "O Trinity, encircle me, for I love you.... To you I lift up my soul." (You can also

pray to each member of the Trinity: "O Abba . . . O Jesu . . . O Parakletos . . .")

Soul Talk

1. As you read Frank Laubach's story, what were your thoughts and feelings?
2. How does it affect you to relate to God as a Trinity of Father, Son, and Spirit, each putting a spotlight of love and glory on the others?
3. What is your experience with contemplative prayer that's quiet and uses few words or seeks to simply be in God's presence?
4. How were you inspired or challenged by the Scriptures on Transforming Union?
5. What was your experience with using David's consecration prayer to devote your whole self (all your personality functions) to God?

10

Friends on the Journey

Understanding and sharing our stories of faith facilitates true community.

Jesus said, "I have come to give you everything in abundance, more than you expect—life in its fullness until you overflow!"

John 10:10 TPT

The best baseball players are voted into the Hall of Fame and their picture is put on a wall with all the great ones. Other sports and the arts have similar museums to enshrine their superstars. The Bible, however, has the Hall of *Faith*, and it features not superstars but *ordinary people* who had great faith in God (Heb. 11). Here faith does not mean believing for and receiving miraculous answers to prayer—*it's persevering in the ups and downs of life to keep loving God and people because you trust that the Lord is beautiful, good, just, and loving all the time.*

One of the people featured in the Hall of Faith is Abraham. His story is like yours. He experienced consolation and desolation, failure and success, and through it all he had the opportunity to grow spiritually. In the table below we outline the defining moments in his journey of grace and identify the CHRIST stages he may have experienced along the way.

Abraham's Journey Map				
TIME (GENESIS)	CONSOLATION EVENTS	DESOLATION EVENTS	SPIRITUAL THEMES	CHRIST STAGE
11:27–12:20	Family blessings Called to promised land	Famine Lies about his wife	Follow the Lord	C
13:1–14:16	Builds altar	Conflict with Lot War	Worship the Lord	H
14:17–24	Blessed by Melchizedek		Tithing	R
15:1–21	God's promise renewed	Infertility	Faith in God	R
16:1–15		Still no children Conflict with Sarah Child (Ishmael) via servant	Self-help is no help Wait for the Lord	The Wall
17:1–19:38	"Father of nations" Three angelic visitors	Sodom and Gomorrah Intercedes for Lot	Trust in God's power	I
20:1–21:34	Promised son (Isaac) Prays for Abimelech's healing	Lies and repents Family conflict	God's promises come true	I
22:1–16		Sacrifices Isaac on altar	Surrender to God	The Wall
22:17–23:20	Lord saves Isaac	Sarah dies	Lord gives new life	I
24:1–67	Finds wife for Isaac		Mentors his servant	S
25:1–8	Family blessings Dies in peace		Legacy of faith	T

Often we have trouble connecting with people who are two CHRIST stages apart from us. Yet, if we're abiding in Christ in our stage, then we will have empathy and respect for people in other stages, especially the earlier ones. We'll be able to travel back, so to speak, to feel and express the spirituality of stages we experienced in the past. This is an important lesson from Abraham's life: true community includes being in relationship with people who are in different stages of the journey than you are.[1] He appreciated people who were more spiritually mature than he was (Melchizedek and the three visitors), those who were less mature (his nephew Lot, children, and servants), and those who were of similar maturity (his wife Sarah). As Paul insists, "In Christ's family there can be no division. . . . You are all equal. That is, we are all in a common relationship with Jesus Christ" (Gal. 3:28 MSG).

When people seek to understand and accept one another, it fosters unity and growth in Christ. It even promotes positive changes in our brain circuitry that promote emotional and relational connection, decreased anxiety, and increased compassion.[2] What might this look like in your church group or other community? Here are some ideas for supporting one another in different CHRIST stages:

- Friends can offer empathy and encouragement to one another to understand their current stage and follow Jesus in it.
- Disciple-makers can recommend key Scriptures, disciplines, and ministry activities that fit different stages.
- Pastors can speak to the differing challenges and needs at each CHRIST stage so no one in church is left out.
- Worship leaders can select songs that speak to themes in various stages.[3]
- Church leaders can ask people at different stages to share their grace stories.

- Bible teachers can apply their text to the needs people have at particular stages.
- A great way for you and your friends to share your life stories and growth in the CHRIST stages is to make Journey Maps. Below we show you how to do that.

Soul Care Practice

Making a Journey Map

I (Kristi) invite you to reflect on your faith story. Mapping your journey with Jesus at different ages helps you to better appreciate God's presence and activity in your life. It helps you to track your journey through the CHRIST stages of emotional and spiritual growth with their consolations, desolations, and life lessons. It also guides you in your spiritual formation and soul care going forward. Then you can share your Journey Map with a friend or small group and pray for one another.

Jesus says to us, "Come with me by yourselves to a quiet place and get some rest" (Mark 6:31). A fun and encouraging way to make your Journey Map and share it with friends is on retreat or in a set-apart meeting.

To help you complete your map you can draw ideas and inspiration from Abraham's journey above and my map below.[4]

Here are the steps to make your map:

1. Gather several large sheets of paper, a pencil, and an eraser (to make adjustments). You may also want colored pencils or markers and/or sticky notes of different colors.

2. Pray for the Holy Spirit to illumine your memory and give you insights.

3. At the top of your map, divide your history into ages or life periods.

4. For each age, plot key consolation events (e.g., God's blessings).

5. For each age, plot key desolation events (e.g., lack of blessing).

6. For each age, plot key spiritual insights you discovered.

7. Plot your CHRIST stages. (You may not have experienced some yet.)

Soul Talk

1. What do you appreciate about Abraham's or Kristi's faith journey?

2. Which CHRIST stage are you currently experiencing, and what is this like for you?

3. What is a key life lesson the Lord has taught you in your journey?

4. If you haven't yet made a Journey Map, how do you feel about this? If you have made one, what has been the fruit of this?

5. How does it feel for you to share your spiritual story with others?

Kristi's Journey Map[5]

	CHILDHOOD	SCHOOL YEARS	YOUNG ADULT	FAMILY LIFE	MIDLIFE	
	C STAGE	H STAGE	R STAGE	R STAGE	I STAGE	S STAGE
CONSOLATIONS	• Christian family • Received car & prayer • Bible stories • Trusted Christ • Family vacations • Extended family	• Belonging at church • Church choir & VBS • Baptized • Praise songs • Scripture memory • Christian camps • Discipled by mom & youth leader • Leading at church • Christian conference	• Christian university • Discipleship community • Served as chaplain, RA & head RA • Community service • Mission trips • Psychology classes • Received therapy	• Married Bill • Birth of 3 children • Church life & ministry • Bill's renewal • Discipling children • God's provision	• Kids to Christian colleges • Retreats • Healing prayer • Spiritual books • Spiritual friends • Enneagram • Free of shame bully • Adult children's successes • Intimacy with Jesus	• Soul Shepherding ministry • Using my gifts (not hiding) • Sabbatical with Bill • Thankful for my grace story • Venturing on God • Ministry as a wounded healer • Investing in others
DESOLATIONS	• Surgery as infant • Lack of empathy	• Bullied and teased • Legalistic messages on hell • Moved to California • Friend died • Sisters to college • Parents in conflict • Acne • No friends	• "Too sensitive" • Abusive boyfriend • Sick for 6 months • Depressed	THE WALL • Lonely in marriage • Family stress • Juggling too many balls • Shamed by Christian speaker • Chronic neck pain • Doubt/dark nights • Recession • Ministry trials • Daughter's health problems • Dad & grandparents died	• Let go of adult children • Changing churches • Menopause	• Hysterectomy • Challenges of ministry • Death to self • Judged by church elders • Surrender to grow ministry

Appendix

Models of the Journey

Over the centuries there have been a number of models describing the stages in spiritual and psychological development. The chart on the facing page compares eight stage theories with Soul Shepherding's CHRIST stages.

Stages of Development

Soul Shepherding	John the Apostle (Bible)	Orthodox (ancient)	Teresa's Mansions (sixteenth century)	Erik Erikson's Psychosocial Stages	James Fowler, Stages of Faith	Brueggemann, Praying the Psalms	M. Scott Peck	Hagberg and Guelich, The Critical Journey
				1. Trust vs. Mistrust; 2. Autonomy vs. Shame & Doubt	0. Undifferentiated Faith		Chaotic	
Confidence in Christ	Spiritual Children	Awakening	1. New Beginnings; 2. Divided Life	3. Initiative vs. Guilt; 4. Industry vs. Inferiority	1. Intuitive & Projective	Orientation	Fundamental	1. Recognition of God
Help in Discipleship			3a. Following Jesus	5. Identity vs. Role Confusion	2. Mythic & Literal			2. Life of Discipleship
Responsibilities in Ministry					3. Synthetic & Conventional			3. Productive Life
The Wall (Transition)	Spiritual Young Adults	Purgation	3b. Aridity			Disorientation	Questioner	4. Journey Inward; The Wall
Inner Journey			4. Discovering the Love of Jesus; 5. Longing for Oneness with God	6. Intimacy vs. Isolation	4. Individuative & Reflective			
Spirit-Led Ministry	Spiritual Fathers and Mothers	Illumination	6a. Dark Nights of the Soul; 6b. Passion for God	7. Generativity vs. Stagnation	5. Conjunctive	Reorientation	Mystic	5. Journey Outward
Transforming Union		Union	7. Life of Love in the Trinity	8. Integrity vs. Despair	6. Universalizing			6. Life of Love

Notes

Introduction

1. James K. A. Smith, *You Are What You Love: The Spiritual Power of Habit* (Grand Rapids: Brazos, 2016), 38.
2. See journeyofthesoul.org.
3. Anonymous, *The Way of a Pilgrim*, trans. R. M. French (New York: Harper, 1952), 1.
4. Dallas Willard, *Life Without Lack: Living in the Fullness of Psalm 23* (Nashville: Thomas Nelson, 2018), 24.
5. Dallas Willard, *The Divine Conspiracy: Rediscovering Our Hidden Life in Christ* (San Francisco: Harper, 1997), 362.

Chapter 1 Shepherding Your Soul

1. Richard Foster, *Prayer: Finding the Heart's True Home* (San Francisco: Harper, 1992), 52–53.
2. Henri Nouwen, *In the Name of Jesus: Reflections on Christian Leadership* (New York: Crossroad, 1989), 57.
3. Nouwen, *In the Name of Jesus*, 73.
4. Foster, *Prayer*, 62–63.
5. Teresa of Ávila, *Interior Castle*, trans. E. Allison Peers (New York: Doubleday, 2004), 3–4, 13. (Teresa is also called Teresa of Jesus.)
6. Dallas Willard, *Renovation of the Heart: Putting on the Character of Christ* (Colorado Springs: NavPress, 2002), 32–39.
7. Anonymous, *The Way of a Pilgrim*, trans. R. M. French (New York: Harper, 1952).
8. Jesus said, "I am the way and the truth and the life" (John 14:6), and his disciples were called followers of "the Way" (Acts 9:2; 19:9, 23; 22:4).

9. There are other developmental models of growing faith in the Bible. Moses recorded the stages of Israel's journey of deliverance from slavery, wandering in the wilderness, and entering the promised land (Num. 33). Psalms 23, 84, 91, and 120–134 (the Pilgrim Psalms) illustrate our journey. Peter identified a progression of steps for growing in faith-based knowledge (2 Pet. 1:3–7).

10. See the appendix of key models of spiritual or psychological development from ancient times to the present day and how they compare to our CHRIST stages.

11. See journeyofthesoul.org for free Soul Shepherding playlists of songs for each of the CHRIST stages and The Wall. Listening to these songs helps you to appreciate and celebrate the themes, rhythms, and tones of each stage. You'll also find resources for small groups, sermons, retreats, and personal devotions.

12. Usually we use *stages* of faith or growth because it's the conventional term. We intend for it to refer to overlapping *phases* of emotional and spiritual development that we move in and out of.

13. Henri Nouwen, *The Return of the Prodigal Son: A Story of Homecoming* (New York: Image, 1994), 56.

14. In John 1, Jesus is called "the Word" (*logos* in Greek), and this can be translated as "Living Expression" or "Blueprint" (TPT).

15. Bill Gaultiere, "The Christian Psychotherapist as a Transitional Object to God," *Journal of Psychology and Theology* 18, no. 2 (1990): 132–34.

16. Rob Moll, *What Your Body Knows About God: How We Are Designed to Connect, Serve, and Thrive* (Downers Grove, IL: InterVarsity, 2014), 15.

17. Matthew 11:28; John 4:13–14; 7:37–39.

18. Hebrews 13:5; Matthew 28:20; Luke 12:32.

19. Kristi Gaultiere, "Selah: Psalm 23," *Soul Talks* (podcast), episode 112, https://www.soulshepherding.org/podcast/selah-psalm-23/. See also Bill Gaultiere, "Journey: Visual Devotions in Psalm 23," https://www.soulshepherding.org/store/journey-visual-devotions-in-psalm-23/.

Chapter 2 Grace for Your Journey

1. Laura is not her real name, and identifying details have been changed. This is the case for the other stories of people in this book, unless indicated otherwise.

2. Adapted from Frank Lake, *Clinical Theology: A Theological and Psychological Basis to Clinical Pastoral Care* (London: DLT, 1986), 70.

3. *Poiēma* in Greek.

4. Malachi 4:2; John 5:40.

5. Brennan Manning, *All Is Grace: A Ragamuffin Memoir* (Colorado Springs: David C. Cook, 2011), 107.

6. Brennan Manning, *The Relentless Tenderness of Jesus* (Grand Rapids: Revell, 2004), 146–47.

7. Manning, *Relentless Tenderness*, 31.

8. See Romans 8:39 MSG.

9. Dallas Willard, *The Great Omission: Reclaiming Jesus's Essential Teachings on Discipleship* (San Francisco: Harper, 2006), 61.

10. Willard, *Great Omission*, 166.

11. This includes Luke and Acts, which Paul influenced.

12. Willard, *Great Omission*, 62.

13. "The Kingdom of the Heavens" is plural because there are levels to the heavens and that's the literal translation of most Bible references (see Young's Literal Translation). We capitalize this and "the Kingdom of God" to emphasize that even though it's invisible on earth it's a real place to live.

14. Ignatius, *The Spiritual Exercises of Saint Ignatius*, trans. George E. Ganss, SJ (Chicago: Loyola Press, 1992).

15. The psychological term for this is *object constancy*.

16. Acts 16:7; Philippians 1:19.

17. Dallas Willard, "A Cup Running Over," *The Art and Craft of Biblical Preaching*, ed. Haddon Robinson and Craig Brian Larson (Grand Rapids: Zondervan, 2005), 71.

18. Gene Edwards, *The Prisoner in the Third Cell* (Carol Stream, IL: Tyndale, 1991).

19. Some insights into Paul's story are from John Pollock, *Apostle: A Life of Paul* (Wheaton: Victor Books, 1985) and Gene Edwards, *Revolution: The Story of the Early Church* (Sargent, GA: SeedSowers, 1974).

20. Compare Acts 7:48 and 17:24.

21. Luke cites the names of Barnabas and Paul together twenty-one times in the book of Acts. Barnabas is mentioned first seven times, then there is a back-and-forth with Paul in the lead ten times and Barnabas four times.

22. After his mission to Cyprus he began using his Roman name, Paul, rather than his Jewish name, Saul (Acts 13:9). Saul means "sought-after" and connotes being ego-driven, and Paul means "little" and connotes humility in God's service. This is the journey of every Christ-follower.

23. Paul was rejected by his fellow Jews in Acts 9:29; 13:50; 14:5; 18:5–12; and Romans 9:3.

24. See Acts 9:23, 29; 14:19; 16:19–24; 20:3; 21:30; 23:10–12; 25:3; 26:32–27:1; 27:14–20; Romans 9:1–4; 2 Corinthians 11:24–25; 2 Timothy 4:10–16.

25. Paul was a bivocational pastor who worked very hard (2 Thess. 3:8). See also Acts 18:1–3; 20:33–35; Philippians 4:14–16.

26. See 1 Corinthians 10:13; 2 Corinthians 12:7–9; Ephesians 6:10–12; and 1 Thessalonians 2:18.

27. See 2 Corinthians 11:3; Philippians 1:21; 3:7–14.

28. Paul did not gain prominence as a Christian leader until he was about fifty-three years old, when he started going on church-planting missions (Acts 13) and wrote letters to those churches.

29. See Galatians 3:28–29 and Colossians 3:11. Also, Paul influenced Luke's Gospel, which emphasizes Jesus' gospel for gentiles, the poor, women, widows, lepers, and "sinners."

30. First Corinthians 2:1–5 and Philippians 3:1–7 give Paul's story. Romans 8:5–9; Galatians 3:3; 5:16–26 feature Paul's teaching.

31. Acts 9:3–12; 16:9–10; 18:9–10; 22:17–21; 23:11; 27:23–24; 2 Corinthians 12:1–4; Galatians 1:11–12.

32. See Acts 16:1–3; 1 Timothy 1:1–2.

33. See Acts 15:37–39; 2 Timothy 4:10–16.

Chapter 3 The C Stage: Confidence in Christ

1. "Chutzpah" is Yiddish slang for having the nerve to take a risk and act with bold faith in God.

2. James Fowler, *Stages of Faith: The Psychology of Human Development and the Quest for Meaning* (San Francisco: Harper, 1981), 132–34.

3. Erik Erikson, *Childhood and Society* (New York: Norton, 1985), 247–58.

4. Gary Wilkinson, *John Newton* (Worcester, PA: Vision Video, 2006).

5. C. S. Lewis, *Surprised by Joy: The Shape of My Early Life* (New York: Harper, 2017), 279.

6. George Barna, "Survey: Christians Are Not Spreading the Gospel," November 30, 2017. Referenced by William F. Cox Jr. and Robert A. Peck in "Christian Education as Discipleship Formation," June 7, 2018, *Christian Education Journal* 15, no. 2 (2018): 243–61.

7. Teresa of Ávila, *Interior Castle*, trans. E. Allison Peers (New York: Doubleday, 2004), 16.

8. Teresa, *Interior Castle*, 24.

9. Lamentations 3:22–23.

10. Tim Clinton and Gary Sibcy, *Attachments: Why You Love, Feel, and Act the Way You Do* (Brentwood, TN: Integrity, 2002), 148–49.

11. Jeff McCrory, translation from the Hebrew, personal email, November 16, 2019.

12. Rob Moll, *What Your Body Knows About God: How We Are Designed to Connect, Serve, and Thrive* (Downers Grove, IL: InterVarsity, 2014), 52–56.

13. René Spitz, "Hospitalism: An Inquiry into the Genesis of Psychiatric Conditions in Early Childhood," *Psychoanalytic Study of the Child* 1 (1945): 53–74.

14. Moll, *What Your Body Knows About God*, 67.

15. A. W. Tozer, *The Knowledge of the Holy* (San Francisco: Harper, 1961), 1.

16. Tim Jennings, *The God-Shaped Brain* (Downers Grove, IL: InterVarsity, 2013).

17. Marion Wheeler, *His Face: Images of Christ in Art* (New York: Smithmark, 1996).

18. See Mark 5:2, 6, 14; 6:33, 55; 9:15, 25; 10:17; 15:36.

19. Fowler, *Stages of Faith*, 132–34.

20. In Israel's journey, they're slaves in Egypt till Yahweh delivers them (Exod. 13–14) and promises, "I am the Lord, who heals you" (Exod. 15:26). In the desert the Lord provides them manna and quail to eat and water from the rock to drink (Exod. 16). Then at Mount Sinai the Lord speaks the commandments (Exod. 20).

21. Sanjiv Chopra and Gina Vild, "Fake It Until You Make It," *Psychology Today*, August 12, 2018, https://www.psychologytoday.com/us/blog/your-life-s-purpose /201808/fake-it-until-you-make-it.

22. Bill Gaultiere, "Breath Prayer Guides," https://www.soulshepherding.org /store/breath-prayer-guides/.

23. Zephaniah 3:17.

24. Bill Gaultiere, "Jesus Smiles at You!," https://www.soulshepherding.org/ jesus-smiles/.

25. Gaultiere, "Breath Prayer Guides."

Chapter 4 The H Stage: Help in Discipleship

1. Rob Moll, *What Your Body Knows About God: How We Are Designed to Connect, Serve, and Thrive* (Downers Grove, IL: InterVarsity, 2014), 178.

2. Teresa of Ávila, *Interior Castle*, trans. E. Allison Peers (New York: Doubleday, 2004), 27.

3. James Fowler, *Stages of Faith: The Psychology of Human Development and the Quest for Meaning* (San Francisco: Harper, 1981), 135–36.

4. Walter Brueggemann, *Praying the Psalms: Engaging Scripture and the Life of the Spirit* (Eugene, OR: Cascade Books, 2007), 2–4.

5. The blessings and limitations of the Law are taught in Romans 7:10–12; 2 Corinthians 3:9; and Galatians 3:24.

6. Matthew 28:1–10; John 20:1–18; Acts 1:14.

7. Dallas Willard, *Hearing God* (Downers Grove, IL: InterVarsity, 1999), 10.

8. The Greek word for mind (*nous*), as in Romans 12:2, includes thoughts and emotions. *Thayer's Greek Lexicon*, s.v. "3563: *nous*," Bible Hub, https://biblehub.com/thayers/3563.htm.

9. Moll, *What Your Body Knows About God*, 57–58.

10. Bill Gaultiere, *Your Best Life in Jesus' Easy Yoke: Rhythms of Grace to De-Stress and Live Empowered* (Irvine, CA: Soul Shepherding, 2016), 85–104.

11. Chris Webb, *The Fire of the Word: Meeting God on Holy Ground* (Downers Grove, IL: InterVarsity, 2011), 32.

12. Raymond C. Ortlund, *Lord, Make My Life a Miracle!* (Ventura, CA: Regal, 1974), 65.

13. Gaultiere, *Your Best Life in Jesus' Easy Yoke*, 30.

14. Gaultiere, *Your Best Life in Jesus' Easy Yoke*, 10.

15. Dietrich Bonhoeffer, *Psalms: The Prayer Book of the Bible* (Minneapolis: Augsburg, 1970), 16.

16. Quoted in Walter Trobisch, *Martin Luther's Quiet Time* (Downers Grove, IL: InterVarsity, 1975), 1.

17. Martin Luther, *A Simple Way to Pray* (Louisville: Westminster John Knox, 2000), 18.

18. Luther, *Simple Way*, 30.

19. Luther, *Simple Way*, 33.

20. Luther, *Simple Way*, 56.

21. Dallas Willard set this example in his Doctor of Ministry class and in *The Divine Conspiracy: Rediscovering Our Hidden Life in Christ* (San Francisco: Harper, 1997), 269.

Chapter 5 The R Stage: Responsibilities in Ministry

1. R. Thomas Ashbrook, *Mansions of the Heart: Exploring the Seven Stages of Spiritual Growth* (San Francisco: Jossey-Bass, 2009), 92. Teresa of Jesus' stages are listed in the appendix.

2. Anonymously adapted from John Wesley's sermon on "The Use of Money."

3. James Fowler, *Stages of Faith: The Psychology of Human Development and the Quest for Meaning* (San Francisco: Harper, 1981), 151–73.

4. Erik Erikson, *Childhood and Society* (New York: Norton, 1985), 261–63.

5. In Acts, Paul/Saul is named 221 times, Peter/Simon is named 79 times, and John is named 20 times.

6. Five times John anonymously identifies himself as the beloved disciple of Jesus (John 13:23; 19:26; 20:2; 21:7, 20).

7. Attributed to Martin Luther. Source unknown.

8. The gifts of the Spirit from 1 Corinthians 12:7–11 are also important for ministry.

9. For more discussion see Bill Gaultiere, "Women as Pastors, Elders, and Leaders in Bible-Based Churches," Soul Shepherding, https://www.soulshepherding.org/women-pastors-elders-leaders-bible-based-christian-churches/.

10. Bill Gaultiere, *Your Best Life in Jesus' Easy Yoke: Rhythms of Grace to De-Stress and Live Empowered* (Irvine, CA: Soul Shepherding, 2016), 149–70.

11. From Robert A. Johnston and Jerry M. Ruhl, *Balancing Heaven and Earth* (New York: HarperCollins, 1998), 173–74, quoted in Brennan Manning, *All Is Grace* (Colorado Springs: David C. Cook, 2011), 159.

12. Dallas Willard, "Spirituality and Ministry," Doctor of Ministry class for Fuller Theological Seminary, June 2012.

13. Quoted by Jan Johnson in *When the Soul Listens* (Colorado Springs: NavPress, 1999), 145.

Chapter 6 Transition: Through The Wall

1. *St. Benedict's Rule for Monasteries* (Collegeville, MN: Order of Saint Benedict, 1948), 73.

2. Henri Nouwen's paraphrase of Psalm 23:4, "Light in the Darkness," Henri Nouwen Society, December 22, 2018, https://henrinouwen.org/meditation/light-in-the-darkness/.

3. James Fowler, *Stages of Faith: The Psychology of Human Development and the Quest for Meaning* (San Francisco: Harper, 1981), 181.

4. Janet O. Hagberg and Robert A. Guelich, *The Critical Journey: Stages in the Life of Faith* (Salem, WI: Sheffield, 2005), 115.

5. M. Scott Peck, *The Different Drum: Community Making and Peace* (New York: Simon and Schuster, 1987), 151.

6. Chapter 8 unpacks the Dark Night of the Soul.

7. Richard Rohr, *Falling Upward* (San Francisco: Jossey-Bass, 2011), 32.

8. Walter Brueggemann, *Praying the Psalms: Engaging Scripture and the Life of the Spirit* (Eugene, OR: Cascade Books, 2007), 19–26.

9. In Titus 1:6–9 (MSG) the relational leadership traits most closely tied to EQ include not short-tempered, not a drunk, not a bully, welcoming people, helpful, and having a good grip on self.

10. From "The Apprentice Prayer" by Bill Gaultiere, *Your Best Life in Jesus' Easy Yoke: Rhythms of Grace to De-Stress and Live Empowered* (Irvine, CA: Soul Shepherding, 2016), 2.

11. David Kinnaman, "Church Dropouts Have Risen to 64%—But What About Those Who Stay?," September 4, 2019, https://www.barna.com/research/resilient-disciples/.

12. David Kinnaman, "Six Reasons Why Young Christians Leave Church," September 27, 2011, https://www.barna.com/research/six-reasons-young-christians -leave-church/.

13. Kinnaman, "Church Dropouts."

14. Greg L. Hawkins and Cally Parkinson, *Reveal* (Barrington, IL: Willow Creek, 2007), 47–64.

15. The Hebrew word *naphash* in 2 Samuel 16:14 is translated as "refreshed" and is derived from *nephesh*, which is translated as "soul." My term "re-soul" combines the two. See Strong's Concordance, s.v. "5314: naphash," Bible Hub, https://biblehub.com/hebrew/5314.htm.

16. Referenced in Rohr, *Falling Upward*, 73.

17. C. S. Lewis, *A Grief Observed* (New York: Bantam Books, 1980), 6.

18. Lewis, *A Grief Observed*, 4–5.

19. James F. Masterson, MD, seminar on "Treating Borderline Patients," 1999.

20. Quoted in James M. Houston, "The Prayer Life of C. S. Lewis," *Knowing and Doing* (Summer 2006): 3, https://www.cslewisinstitute.org/webfm_send /646.

21. Scott Peck's third stage of faith, Skeptic, correlates with The Wall and comes before a final stage called Mystic. He describes mystical faith as appreciating the mystery of God, emptying yourself of prejudice, accepting and including people, and transcending normal human limits. See *The Different Drum*, 148–62.

22. C. S. Lewis, *The Problem of Pain* (New York: Macmillan, 1962), 93.

23. Lewis, *A Grief Observed*, 80–81, 83.

24. Bill Gaultiere, *Unforsaken: With Jesus on the Stations of the Cross* (Irvine, CA: Soul Shepherding: 2016). See UnforsakenGuide.com.

25. Peter Kreeft, *Christianity for Modern Pagans: Pascal's Pensées* (San Francisco: Ignatius, 1966), 172.

26. John of the Cross, *The Essential Writings: John of the Cross* (San Francisco: Harper, 2009), 90–91.

27. Sabbath is the first day of the week (Matt. 28:1; Acts 20:7). See also Gaultiere, *Your Best Life in Jesus' Easy Yoke*, 139–148.

28. From the movie *Christopher Robin* (Walt Disney Pictures, 2018), inspired by A. A. Milne's *Winnie the Pooh*.

29. See *Journey: Visual Devotions in Psalm 23* and other visual devotions by Bill Gaultiere on SoulShepherding.org.

30. *Remez* is a Semitic word that means "hint." The idea is that using a first or beloved line from a well-known poem, song, or reading can invoke the whole. Doug Greenwold, "Forsaken or Abandoned? A Passion Week Reflection," Preserving Bible Times, https://preservingbibletimes.org/wp-content/uploads/2014/03 /Reflection.Forsaken.pdf.

31. Gaultiere, *Unforsaken*.

32. Brueggemann, *Praying the Psalms*, 8–15.

Chapter 7 The I Stage: Inner Journey

1. Teresa of Ávila, *Interior Castle*, trans. E. Allison Peers (New York: Doubleday, 2004), 54.

2. James Fowler, *Stages of Faith: The Psychology of Human Development and the Quest for Meaning* (San Francisco: Harper, 1981), 174–83.

3. James Finley, "Dreaming Compassion," February 24, 2017, Center for Action and Contemplation, https://cac.org/dreaming-compassion-2017-02-24/.

4. Psychology of religion author James Fowler calls this "recapitulation." See Fowler, *Stages of Faith*, 288–91.

5. Neurological studies cited by Rob Moll, *What Your Body Knows About God: How We Are Designed to Connect, Serve, and Thrive* (Downers Grove, IL: InterVarsity, 2014), 119–20.

6. Clare of Assisi, *Francis and Clare: The Complete Works*, trans. Regis J. Armstrong and Ignatius C. Brady (New York: Paulist, 1982), 204–5. (This has been lightly edited by Bill Gaultiere.)

7. Bill Gaultiere, "How to Feel Your Emotions with Jesus," Soul Shepherding, https://www.soulshepherding.org/how-to-feel-your-emotions-with-jesus/. These are not just emotions but conditions of our whole being (or soul) that involve our body, thoughts, will, and social connections.

8. Of course, it's also important to admire and bond with Jesus the thinker.

9. David Stoop and Jan Stoop, *SMART Love: How Improving Your Emotional Intelligence Will Transform Your Marriage* (Grand Rapids: Revell, 2017), 9–13, based on research by Daniel Goleman in 1995.

10. John Wesley, *John and Charles Wesley: Selected Writings and Hymns*, ed. Frank Whaling (Mahwah, NJ: Paulist, 1981), 107.

11. James Gilchrist Lawson, *The Deeper Experiences of Famous Christians* (Uhrichsville, OH: Barbour, 1999), 8.

12. We can experience the Holy Spirit's blessing in any stage. In the I Stage there's an immersive experience of God's love that brings spiritual renewal and power.

13. C. S. Lewis, *Mere Christianity* (San Francisco: Harper, 2001), 176–77.

14. Jeanne Guyon, *Experiencing the Depths of Jesus Christ* (Jacksonville: SeedSowers, 1981), ix–2.

15. Psalm 147:4; Romans 8:15; James 4:12.

16. Brennan Manning, *Abba's Child: The Cry of the Heart for Intimate Belonging* (Colorado Springs: Navpress, 1994), 64–65.

17. Henri Nouwen, *Life of the Beloved* (New York: Crossroad, 2002), 37.

18. Bill Gaultiere, "The Jesus Burn: A Blessed Experience of God's Peace," Soul Shepherding, https://www.soulshepherding.org/the-jesus-burn-a-blessed-experience-of-gods-presence/.

19. Lewis, *Mere Christianity*, 176–77.

20. C. S. Lewis, *Surprised by Joy: The Shape of My Early Life* (New York: Harper, 2017), 23.

21. Teresa, *Interior Castle*, 117.

22. David urges us to "take heart" (Ps. 27:14; 31:24), as does Jesus (Matt. 9:2, 22; John 16:33).

23. C. Austin Miles, "In the Garden" (1912).

24. Henri Nouwen, "The Disciplines of the Beloved," sermon at the Crystal Cathedral in Garden Grove, CA, in 1992.

25. Manning, *Abba's Child*, 168.

26. Bill Gaultiere, "Ignatian Meditation Guides" and "Lectio Divina Guides," available from SoulShepherding.org.

27. Bill Gaultiere, "Hungry Heart Scriptures," Soul Shepherding, https://www.soulshepherding.org/hungry-heart-scriptures/. Instead of being grumpy or feeling deprived when we fast, like the Pharisees of Jesus' day, we can feast with joy on God's Word (Matt. 6:16–18).

28. Bill Gaultiere, "Reading Classic Devotional Books," Soul Shepherding, https://www.soulshepherding.org/reading-classic-devotional-books/. This article lists about fifty top classics.

29. Dallas Willard, *The Divine Conspiracy: Rediscovering Our Hidden Life in Christ* (San Francisco: Harper, 1997), 295–97, 323–41.

30. Frank Laubach, *Prayer: The Mightiest Force in the World* (Grand Rapids: Revell, 1946), 72–74.

31. The Gospel of Mark takes only one hour and fifteen minutes to read or listen to on a Bible app. You can also watch Mark's Gospel (NIV) performed by Max McLean, available for free on the Fellowship for Performing Arts YouTube channel, https://www.youtube.com/user/FPAVideos/playlists.

32. Paul and Luke traveled together. The Gospel of Luke and Paul's letters have a similar emphasis on God's grace being for all people, including outsiders.

33. Colossians 1:15–20, 22, 27; 2:3, 6–7; 3:17 (MSG).

Chapter 8 The S Stage: Spirit-Led Ministry

1. Joe Johnson, Heart of the Father Ministries, personal conversation.

2. *Parakletos* is the Greek name Jesus gives to Holy Spirit, and it's variously translated as "Friend," "Advocate," "Counselor," and "Helper" (see John 14:16, 26; 15:26; 16:7).

3. James Fowler, *Stages of Faith: The Psychology of Human Development and the Quest for Meaning* (San Francisco: Harper, 1981), 184–98.

4. George Fox, *The Essence of George Fox's Journal*, ed. Hunter Lewis (Edinburg, VA: Axios, 2012), 117.

5. Erik Erikson, *Childhood and Society* (New York: Norton, 1985), 166–68.

6. Being governed by emotional desire or impulsiveness is living from our belly rather than the heavens (Phil. 3:19–21). It's being controlled by the flesh rather than the Spirit (Gal. 5:19–22).

7. Teresa of Ávila, *Interior Castle*, trans. E. Allison Peers (New York: Doubleday, 2004), 116–203.

8. Thomas Kelly, *A Testament of Devotion* (San Francisco: Harper, 1992), 46.

9. The psalmist often prays about feeling distant from God (e.g., 10:1; 13:1; 22:1–2; 27:9; 30:7; 44:24; 69:17; 88:14; 102:2; 104:29; 143:7).

10. John of the Cross, *The Essential Writings: John of the Cross* (San Francisco: Harper, 2009), 2.

11. John of the Cross, *Essential Writings*, 4.

12. Teresa, *Interior Castle*, 41, 118.

13. Fox, *The Essence of George Fox's Journal*, 23.

14. F. B. Meyer, *The Secret of Guidance* (Chicago: Moody, 2010), 28–29.

15. Ignatius, *The Spiritual Exercises of Saint Ignatius*, trans. George E. Ganss, SJ (Chicago: Loyola Press, 1992), 77–78.

16. While it is surprising to many people, the Lord guides us not only through our reason but also through dreams or reflections at night (Ps. 16:7), heart desires (Ps. 37:4), peace in our heart and mind (Phil. 4:6–7), and conversations with mutual listening (James 1:19).

17. Nehemiah 9:20; see also Luke 11:13.

18. Personal conversations with Dallas Willard. See his discussion of "abandonment" in *Renovation of the Heart: Putting on the Character of Christ* (Colorado Springs: Navpress, 2002), 150–52.

19. For instance, study Moses by the burning bush (Exod. 3:2), little Samuel lying in bed (1 Sam. 3:3–7), Elisha listening to the harpist (2 Kings 3:15), Elizabeth feeling the baby leap in her womb (Luke 1:41–45), and Ananias being called to minister to Paul (Acts 9:11).

20. John of the Cross, *Essential Writings*, 58.

21. Dallas Willard, *Hearing God* (Downers Grove, IL: InterVarsity, 1999), 175–77.

22. Teresa, *Interior Castle*, 134–39.

23. Teresa, *Interior Castle*, 157.

24. Teresa, *Interior Castle*, 189.

25. When Jesus delivered the demonized man who lived in the tombs, he told him to share his story (Mark 5:19), but when he healed the deaf and mute man, he told him not to tell anyone (Mark 7:36). Often, it's best to keep a special word, vision, or miracle secret from everyone but close friends for a season.

26. Teresa, *Interior Castle*, 183.

27. Carl Jung, *Memories, Dreams, and Reflections*, ed. Aniela Jaffé (New York: Vintage Books, 1989), 134.

28. Matthew 26:52–54; John 12:27–28; Hebrews 5:7.

29. Henri Nouwen, *The Wounded Healer* (New York: Image, 1972), 44–47.

30. Nouwen, *Wounded Healer*, 100.

31. Rosemary Black, "Glossophobia (Fear of Public Speaking): Are You Glossophobic?," Psycom, September 12, 2019, https://www.psycom.net/glossophobia -fear-of-public-speaking.

32. Bill Gaultiere, *Your Best Life in Jesus' Easy Yoke: Rhythms of Grace to De-Stress and Live Empowered* (Irvine, CA: Soul Shepherding, 2016), 134–35.

33. Jean-Pierre de Caussade, *The Sacrament of the Present Moment* (San Francisco: Harper & Row, 1982), 22.

34. Dallas Willard shared this in a private conversation.

35. This is the spiritual discipline of *statio* practiced by Benedictine monks. See Gaultiere, *Your Best Life in Jesus' Easy Yoke*, 119–25.

36. Kelly, *A Testament of Devotion*, 32, 52, 45.

37. Raymond C. Ortlund, *Lord, Make My Life a Miracle!* (Ventura, CA: Regal, 1974), 2.

38. Kelly, *A Testament of Devotion*, 92.

39. Bill Gaultiere, "Breath Prayer Guides," https://www.soulshepherding.org /store/breath-prayer-guides/.

Chapter 9   The T Stage: Transforming Union

1. Adapted from Teresa of Ávila, *Interior Castle*, trans. E. Allison Peers (New York: Doubleday, 2004), 208.

2. Dallas Willard, *The Divine Conspiracy: Rediscovering Our Hidden Life in Christ* (San Francisco: Harper, 1997), 250.

3. M. Scott Peck, *The Different Drum: Community Making and Peace* (New York: Simon and Schuster, 1987), 165. He suggests one in twenty people reach the final stage of spiritual and psychological growth that he calls "Mystical and Communal."

4. Teresa, *Interior Castle*, 210–12.

5. James Fowler, *Stages of Faith: The Psychology of Human Development and the Quest for Meaning* (San Francisco: Harper, 1981), 200–201.

6. Erik Erikson, *Childhood and Society* (New York: Norton, 1985), 268–69.

7. Jean Guyon, *Madame Jeanne Guyon: Her Autobiography*, ed. Jan Johnson (Jacksonville: SeedSowers, 1998).

8. Brother Lawrence and Frank Laubach, *Practicing His Presence* (Jacksonville: SeedSowers, 1985), 47, 103.

9. Frank C. Laubach, *Man of Prayer* (Syracuse: Laubach Literacy, 1990), 6.

10. Teresa, *Interior Castle*, 214.

11. In the ninety-five verses of Colossians Paul speaks of Jesus Christ eighty-three times! This includes the words "Lord," "Son," and "he" being used to refer to Jesus. It's similar in Paul's other letters.

12. Bernard of Clairvaux, *The Love of God* (Portland, OR: Multnomah, 1983), 158–63.

13. *Perichoresis* (Greek for "dance alongside") is a doctrine developed by the church fathers.

14. Greek language study of *musterion* from Strong's #3466, https://www.study light.org/language-studies/greek-thoughts.html?article=3.

15. Quoted in Lyle Dorsett, *A Passion for God: The Spiritual Journey of A. W. Tozer* (Chicago: Moody, 2008), 138.

16. A. W. Tozer, *The Christian Book of Mystical Verse* (Blacksburg, VA: Wilder, 2011), 11–12.

17. See Robert Frost, "The Road Not Taken," https://www.poetryfoundation .org/poems/44272/the-road-not-taken.

18. A. W. Tozer, *The Radical Cross: Living the Passion of Christ* (Camp Hill, PA: Christian Publications, 2005), 26–28. Note that we have edited Tozer's original text to incorporate gender-neutral pronouns.

19. Jesus' Hebrew name, meaning "He saves."

20. Karen R. Norton, *Frank C. Laubach: One Burning Heart* (Syracuse: Laubach Literacy, 1990), 9–11.

21. Helen M. Roberts, *Champion of the Silent Billion: The Story of Frank C. Laubach* (St. Paul: Macalester, 1961), 11–12.

22. Frank C. Laubach, *Christ Liveth in Me* and *Game with Minutes* (Westwood, NJ: Revell, 1961), 46–48.

23. Frank C. Laubach, *Letters by a Modern Mystic* (New York: Student Volunteer Movement, 1937), 10–11.

24. Norton, *One Burning Heart*, 13–15.

25. Wikipedia, s.v. "Frank Laubach," last modified April 2, 2020, https://en.wiki pedia.org/wiki/Frank_Laubach.

26. Laubach, *Letters by a Modern Mystic*, 12, emphasis added.

27. The general illustration of the Four Waters is from Teresa, *Interior Castle*, 63–64. We added the "No Water" period to represent The Wall.

28. Dorsett, *A Passion for God*, 120.

29. *The Letters: The Epic Life Story of Mother Teresa* (film), directed by William Riead (Big Screen Productions V, 2014).

30. Dallas Willard, *Renovation of the Heart: Putting on the Character of Christ* (Colorado Springs: NavPress, 2002), 10–11.

31. Psalms 16, 27, 42, 63, 77, 84, 86, and 131.

32. John Wesley, *John and Charles Wesley: Selected Writings and Hymns*, ed. Frank Whaling (Mahwah, NJ: Paulist, 1981), 301–2. (This is lightly edited.)

Chapter 10 Friends on the Journey

1. M. Scott Peck, *The Different Drum: Community Making and Peace* (New York: Simon and Schuster, 1987), 156.

2. Curt Thompson, *Anatomy of the Soul* (Carol Stream, IL: Tyndale, 2010), xiv.

3. See journeyofthesoul.org for Soul Shepherding playlists of top contemporary Christian songs for each of the CHRIST stages and The Wall.

4. Bill Gaultiere, "Mapping Your Spiritual Journey," Soul Shepherding, https://www.soulshepherding.org/mapping-your-spiritual-journey/. This article features examples of additional ways to make a Journey Map.

5. Kristi made this Journey Map at age fifty, before experiencing the T Stage.

Drs. Bill and Kristi Gaultiere have been counseling and ministering to people for thirty years. Bill is a psychologist who has served in private practice, co-led a New Life psychiatric day hospital, and pastored churches. Kristi is a marriage and family therapist who has also served in private practice and church ministry. Together they are the founders of Soul Shepherding, a nonprofit ministry to help believers discover their next steps for growing in intimacy with Jesus, emotional health, and loving relationships. Bill and Kristi live in Irvine, California.

Connect with Soul Shepherding

If you were inspired by *Journey of the Soul* and desire to deepen your intimacy with Jesus, we encourage you to connect with Soul Shepherding. Drs. Bill & Kristi Gaultiere founded this ministry to help you thrive with Jesus in life and leadership.

Weekly Blog and Soul Talks Podcast

Follow along as Bill & Kristi invite you into authentic conversations that cultivate emotional and relational health and strengthen your leadership.

Books and Resources

To be encouraged and equipped in your walk with Jesus, check out Bill & Kristi's books and resources. They were written with you in mind, and they're great for personal growth, retreats, and small groups. Our best sellers are *Your Best Life in Jesus' Easy Yoke* and the *Prayer Guides Bundle*.

Soul Shepherding Institute

You can be personally trained by Bill & Kristi in spiritual formation and soul care at the Institute. It features four 5-day retreats in person or online with an option to earn a certificate in the ministry of Spiritual Direction. Bill & Kristi are also available to speak at your church or event.

To learn more, visit
SoulShepherding.org

SOUL
SHEPHERDING

f 🟠 🐦 𝒫 ▶